SYNERGISTIC COLLABORATIONS

Pastoral Care and Church Social Work

Velmarie L. Albertini
and
Jonathan Grenz

University Press of America,® Inc.
Lanham · Boulder · New York · Toronto · Plymouth, UK

"The family of God is the church of the living God. It is the pillar and foundation of the truth."

1 Timothy 3:15 (GW)

"The righteous cares about justice for the poor, but the wicked have no such concern."

Proverbs 29:7 (NIV)

"If you read history, you will find that the Christians who did most for the present world were precisely those who thought most of the next. It is since Christians have largely ceased to think of the other world that they have become so ineffective in this." C.S. Lewis

We dedicate this book to our spouses and children who contributed unconditional love and support throughout the entire writing process. We also dedicate it to pastors and social workers, especially those responding with passion to the call of the Great Commission and in doing so; they seek new ways to collaborate and serve vulnerable people in their society.

CONTENTS

PREFACE

This book embodies the collaborative efforts of two Christian professors who serve in separate, yet very closely related areas of ministry. Dr. Jonathan Grenz currently teaches courses related to Christian leadership and pastoral care at a Christian university in South Florida. Prior to entering the academy, he ministered for over fifteen years as a pastor in both the U.S. and Canada. Dr. Velmarie Albertini has ministered for over fifteen years in another discipline, social work, and has taught social work and Christian social ministry courses at secular and Christian universities in South and Central Florida. Social ministry refers to the organized process used by Christian workers to demonstrate Christ's concern for the spiritual, physical, emotional, mental and relational well-being of individuals, families, and people groups inside and outside the community of faith.[1]

During a brief tenure, while they were both serving on the same faculty in South Florida, Drs. Grenz and Albertini began a series of conversations concerning some of the benefits and challenges that students in their respective disciplines were sure to encounter upon entering Christian ministries. Often in those conversations, they explored the implications of some of the recent social, political and economic changes that were taking place in society and new challenges which such changes might pose for those in Christian ministries. Those conversations also served as the catalyst for further empirical explorations to determine where the two academic disciplines and areas of ministry naturally overlap in churches and communities. The culmination of their years of research, teaching and experiences in ministry has led them to write this book, lending their voices to some of the most salient issues and concerns of our time. When asked why writing this book is so important, Drs. Albertini and Grenz write, Along our ministry and career paths, we have discovered that while some church leaders are rediscovering the efficacies inherent in the church's role of spreading the gospel and ministering to the poor and needy in their communities, many are still struggling to do so.

Some of the authors who have been inspirational and served as trailblazers who have paved the way for our book include Stanley Grenz, a theologian; Tony Campolo, a Christian sociologist; Ronald Sider, a scholar and social activist;

Rick and Kay Warren, pastors and social activists; and Diana Garland, an expert on church social work. All of these authors in some way or another have challenged us to think deeply about the role of the Christian church in the context of Christ's teachings and ministry. It is for that reason that we are now providing readers with this unique opportunity to explore and respond to some of the struggles which churches and church leaders face today. We hope to engage our readers in an ongoing conversation concerning important social issues facing the church and trends in pastoral care ministries and church social work practices, especially given some of the recent social, political and economic changes that have occurred in our society. We begin by asking ourselves and you, the readers, two basic questions.

First, we ask, as part of the American church, are we finding ourselves in more of a proactive or reactive posture in relation to all the socioeconomic and political changes that are taking place around us? Especially with society changing so rapidly, it seems quite legitimate to ask whether churches and church leaders have been more reactive or proactive in responding, for instance, to the economic downturns and crises that are affecting the lives of so many people we encounter. Second, are we as Christians grasping the implications of how some of the socioeconomic and political changes are impacting how we carry out the ministry of the gospel?

It is our position that the Scripture clearly shows that Christ has equipped us as believers with all we need to fulfill our mission in the world. As the New Testament writer of the Book of Matthew puts it in chapter 28, Christ's authority over the church is evident, and His immutable plan concerning the church's role in the world is plain to see:

> ...Jesus... said, "All authority in heaven and on earth has been given to me. Therefore, go and make disciples of all nations [peoples], baptizing them in the name of the Father and of the Son and of the Holy Spirit, and teaching them to obey everything I have commanded you. ...surely, I am with you always, to the very end of the age."[2]

Given Christ's sovereignty and the perfection of His work of salvation, the church is equipped to carry out her responsibility. Still, what does it mean for American churches and church leaders who are challenged on so many fronts to adjust to shifting cultural, social and political landscapes? Our concern is that some church leaders might not comprehend sufficiently implications of some of the political and socioeconomic changes. Some church leaders today are unprepared to assess the changes and therefore to adjust in order to be more effective in ways with which they go about fulfilling their ministry goals and the Great Commission.

Let us consider, for example, ramifications of some of the most significant socioeconomic and political changes, to take place in our society for over half a century. The change occurred in 1996 during the presidency of William Jefferson Clinton. Although the seeds for the change were planted in prior administrations, it was under the Clinton administration that we embarked upon the new socioeconomic era and when, after much planning; the government profoundly altered the social welfare system that addresses the needs of poor and needy people.[3]

In one fell swoop (some say for the better, others the reverse), our nation ended its sixty-year old social welfare system established in the 1930s with President Franklin Roosevelt's "New Deal Plan."[4] Under President Clinton, in more significant ways than many in Christian communities might fully realize, our nation began to decrease the extent to which people are able to turn to federal and state systems for social services. In effect, the reform increased opportunities and frequency for which people in need would be turning to non-government organizations such as churches and parachurch organizations for help.[5] There was yet another change that followed and which was directly and indirectly consequential to how churches do ministries. Here we are referring to developments in the Faith-Based Movement within the government to increase recognition and funding opportunities for non-government organizations that are willing to provide social services in communities where their religious works intersect the lives of poor and needy people.[6]

Researchers who track social, economic and political changes in relation to religious organizations in the U.S. have long recognized that the major paradigm shift taking place in the government meant greater expectations for churches' involvement in addressing people's social service as well as their spiritual needs.[7] Yet few in church leadership and ministries might have grasped the magnitude of the changes related to the passing of what Clinton's administration termed the Personal Responsibility and Work Opportunity Reconciliation Act (PRWORA) and implementation of the Temporary Assistance for Needy Families (TANF). Some of the most radical social service changes to take place in decades were simply termed for the public as "welfare reform". What many might not have realized is the extent to which welfare reform would later be associated with another movement called the Faith-Based Initiative.

The Faith-Based Initiatives became fully established a decade later under the next administration. In 2001, President George W. Bush focused on solidifying laws that permit religious organizations access to federal and state funding to increase their roles and levels of participation in providing social services to the poor.[8] The government essentially has called for more churches to broaden their engagement with the poor, especially those in need of social services— implications of which many in the churches today might not fully comprehend. President Bush, in a sense, called upon Christian communities to recognize or rediscover their historical role of combining social service delivery with spiritual ministries. Let us consider, for example, excerpts taken from an advertisement posted on the government's internet site, which the Bush administration used to advance what they entitled the Faith-Based and Community Initiative. Note that the ad is for a conference held in June of 2008 at the Omni Shoreham Hotel, Connecticut Avenue in Washington, District of Columbia, as in many correspondences, the Bush Administration refers to the Faith-Based Initiatives as a "*quiet revolution*":

> The White House Office of Faith-Based and Community Initiatives will host the Innovations *in Effective Compassion Conference*...The Faith-Based and Community Initiative has sought to transform the way government engages human need. It has worked to place front-line community groups, faith-based charities and other social entrepreneurs at the center of responses to critical issues ranging from addiction, homelessness, prisoner reentry, at-risk youths . . . to HIV/AIDS, orphan care, and malaria around the world. From the first days of his administration, President Bush has pushed the Federal government to support these locally-rooted solutions both at home and abroad, removing barriers to government's support for them, and expanding promising new strategies...Conference attendees including many of the Nation's top researchers, Federal and State officials, social entrepreneurs, and other experts...Presentations...include the latest data, original research, promising innovations, and future opportunities for the "*quiet revolution*" advanced by the Faith-Based and Community Initiative.[9]

In the advertisement, the federal government offered one of many free conferences to train and prepare faith-based groups how to obtain more federal funding and increase their participation in dealing with serious social issues. Church outreach is expected to extend into local communities beyond the "four walls" of the church. While traditionally those serving in pastoral care ministries are likely to be aware of some of the social needs often accompanying spiritual needs of parishioners, it is more likely those experienced in working in secular settings, such as the pastor who transitioned from social-service-type jobs to ministry, or church social workers and other trained counselors, who would be most equipped to address social service needs of individuals, families and communities.

During one of his campaign speech prior to winning the presidential election of 2008, then Senator Barak Obama spoke in favor of the Faith-based Initiative developed under the Clinton and Bush Administrations. Obama endorsed some parts of the initiative that made way for a more level playing field for faith-based organizations to provide social services. He stated, "I still believe it's a good idea to have a partnership between the White House and grassroots groups, both faith-based and secular." However, Obama then went on to say, "If you get a federal grant, you can't use that grant money to proselytize the people you help and you cannot discriminate against them—or against the people you hire—on the basis of their religion." The later part of Obama's statement spells a marked shift from Presidents Clinton's and Bush's views on Charitable Choice or Faith-based initiative. As a constitutional attorney, President Obama might hold different interpretations of the 1964 Civil Rights Act that prohibited discrimination in hiring based on race, sex or religion. Therefore, in his judgment, federal anti-discrimination laws could possibly require even religious organizations that receive any type of federal funding to provide social services to abide by the same hiring practices as secular organizations. Religious organizations would therefore lose the ability to refuse to hire persons whose faith decisions conflict with those of the particular religious organization. Such a shift in the paradigm would present even more challenges for churches and religious organizations that will no doubt be compelled to address the social needs as more and more government social service organizations reduce services. It remains to be seen exactly what the new administration will decide concerning the 1964 Civil Rights Act and the hiring practices of religious organizations that are involved in social service deliveries.

In February 2009, President Obama commissioned a group of grassroots leaders and numerous experts to study effective ways of strengthening partnerships between government and faith-based communities to address social issues. In 2010, the group of leaders and experts wrote a report for President Obama in which they delineated all their recommendations. The report is entitled, *The President's Advisory Council on Faith-Based and Neighborhoods A New Era of Partnership: Report of Recommendations to the President.* The recommendations included best practice ideas, methods of delivering social services, and evaluation of areas for improvement. In the report, the Council urged the new administration to adopt their recommendations, which included new reforms and partnerships aimed at honoring the country's commitment to religious freedom.[10]

Focus of this Book

In light of the *"quiet revolution"* that began under Presidents Clinton and Bush, and the ongoing paradigm shifts under President Obama's administration, it is important for those of us serving in Christian ministries to determine where and how the Bible distinguishes the church's role in spreading the gospel and responding to the poor or hurting people from that of government's role. In so doing, we are sure to discover where the boundaries lie, especially in relation to the New Testament Scripture. By that, we are asking you, the reader, to explore with us whether the church has a mandate from Christ to minister to all and reach out to all people regardless of spiritual, social, economic or political boundaries. We also question whether it is ever pleasing to God for those within the church to withdraw from ministering to any persons, be they within or outside the Christian faith, or even those adversarial to the faith for that matter. The challenge here is to figure out whether an increased measure of grace is to be extended, especially to those outside the faith.[11] Are we, in other words, to expect that it is through our social and spiritual actions that individuals, families and communities around us will realize Christ's perfect work of reconciliation, peace, hope, and love? How should churches respond to calls for more engagement in social service delivery? Is an affirmative response a means of expanding

Christ's message to more communities all across America and thereby creating more communities of Christians? We have been using terms such as "the Church" and "Christian community." Perhaps we should clarify what we mean by those terms before we go further in our discussions.

Just as the word "church," or the phrase "Christian community," brings to mind for us diverse meanings, such might be the case for different readers. Some might choose to associate each term with specific geographic locations in which people gather to worship and serve God. Others might envision elaborate social networks comprised of the ecumenical body of Christ. With either view, the Christian church today is privy to a great window of opportunity at a very pivotal time in our nation's history. It is a time when churches and Christian leaders will directly and indirectly choose to find ways to be more efficacious in contextualizing the Christian gospel with its inherent message of reconciliation, peace, hope, and love for all it touches. On the other hand, some might choose to view this as an era of governmental encroachment upon domains of the church—to which some might opt simply to maintain a stance of cultural disengagement. Either way the term "Christian community" is defined, there are some overarching questions for church leaders to address, such as, Are we, in the churches of the U.S., positioning ourselves to take full advantage of what might be an incredible opportunity that God has afforded us to contextualize the gospel to more people in need? If not, how do we reconcile not seizing the opportunities with consideration for all the directives embedded in the Great Commission? Those overarching questions lead us to the main purpose for writing this book.

Our primary goal in offering this book is to address for our readers all the questions we have raised. Another goal is to offer a resource to those in Christian ministries who are seeking to go beyond the four walls of the church, extend ministries into unfamiliar locales and to contextualize the gospel fully. Our expectation is for there to be significant numbers of Christians experiencing God-given desires as we are to seize the moment offered by the cultural changes. However, they, like us, need information and knowledge on how to reach out effectively to the poor, hurting and dying around them. For instance, many Christians might be uncertain of the degree to which the Bible provides instructions about how we are to serve in secular places. With our extensive background in pastoral care and social work, we hope to provide readers with valuable insights into how to form greater collaboration between our two areas of ministry, especially as each relates to Christ's call to servanthood. In writing this book, we also provide the knowledge-base and frameworks to help to equip today's churches to spread the gospel in new and unchartered territories.

What is most unique about this book is our usage of a combination of case studies, reality dialogue questions, personal experiences and research that broaden our readers' understanding of the synergistic relationship that naturally exists between pastoral care ministry and social work practice. We set out to challenge contemporary perceptions concerning how churches are to go about selecting whom they will help within and outside the church, while at the same time ameliorating existing church ministries. By providing the necessary know-ledge-base and skills to churches, we are taking a fresh look at ways to approach Christian ministries in relation to culture and society. Our prayer is to serve our readers as guides who seek to equip others for ministry and social action.

The Layout of the Book

For our readers' convenience, we have laid out each chapter in a manner that facilitates progressive knowledge and skills building. For instance, in Chapters 1-4 we provide opportunities to explore real social issues encountered in pastor-al care ministries as well as social work practice (e.g. mental health concerns, domestic violence, homelessness, alcoholism, and HIV/AIDS). In Chapter 5, marriage and family issues related to church leaders are addressed using another case study that raises pertinent questions. Chapter 6 deals with approaches some Christian or faith-based organizations employed in response to the country's September 11th crisis. The content of Chapter 7 is strategically arranged in order to prepare readers to understand a new collaborative model that the authors will fully develop in Chapter 8. For instance, the case study in Chapter 7 is unique in that it allows readers to revisit several of the case studies from preceding chap-ters, in order to understand how church leaders might begin to develop and adopt the new collaborative model that blends pastoral care and social work. In Chapter 8, readers have opportunities to analyze all of the steps of the new mod-el that promote synergistic and collaborative relationships between pastors and social workers. Chapter 9 highlights some of the many benefits of having church social workers serve as consultants for various social problems pastors encoun-ter in ministries within local churches. Chapter 10 presents discussions on some of the trends in pastoral care and church social work. In Chapters 11-12, we identify some good resources that are available to American churches and pro-vide job descriptions which help to delineate some qualifications for pastoral care ministers and church social workers who might work towards building more community partnerships as a way of fulfilling the Great Commission. Readers are able to see how, by working collaboratively, they might be better able to fulfill, in our day, Jesus' work concerning spiritual and social needs in the world as proclaimed in Isaiah 60:

> The Spirit of the Sovereign Lord is on me, because the Lord has anointed me to preach good news to the poor. He has sent me to bind up the brokenhearted, to proclaim freedom for the captives and release from darkness for the prisoners.[12]

In the first chapter, we begin with introductory remarks and our first of sev-en case studies, which are composites of experiences we have had in our own ministries and careers. Of course, as with all case studies in this book, the identities of all people we have served are completely omitted. In fact, in none of the case studies did we use any actual cases. We rely solely on composites of our individual and combined experiences.

ACKNOWLEDGEMENTS

We are forever grateful to Professor Irvin Ziemann, a brilliant teacher and editor who embodies the phrase, God-sent. He read through the pages of our manuscript with great diligence. Had it not been for his labor of love and Godly encouragement, the project might not have reached completion.

CHAPTER 1

Pastoral Care and Social Work Practice: Issues Beyond the Pulpit

Introduction

In this first chapter, as in most of the rest, we have provided a pertinent case study to direct our reflections theologically towards spiritual and social dimensions where pastoral care and social work practice might overlap during the daily routines of Christian ministries. We include in our discussions relevant passages from the Bible to address questions concerning the appropriateness of collaborations between pastoral care and social work. For instance, here we present and discuss the first case study involving a family in crisis. We will then examine the case study in light of the writings of the Apostle Paul, who uses the imagery of spiritual clothing to describe godly conduct in ministry to the first century church of Colossae. In his letter, Paul instructs those early followers of Christ to put on a sort of clothing that symbolically depicts seven godly virtues that originate from none other than Christ Himself. Paul writes,

> Therefore, as God's chosen people, holy and dearly loved, clothe yourselves with compassion, kindness, humility, gentleness and patience. Bear with each other and forgive whatever grievances you might have against one another. Forgive as the Lord forgave you. In addition, over all these virtues put on love, which binds them all together in perfect unity.[1]

The new clothing that Paul describes still holds true for us today. God never changes, so all those virtues still apply.[2] God's desire is for us, His children, to adorn ourselves in His virtues so that we might appear more like Him and so those around us might experience God through us. Paul also challenges his readers to show those virtues especially to others who are in need of the benefits of each virtue. Let us now turn our attention to the family described in the case study below. Theirs is a story that challenges us to ask, Which of the seven virtues are they most in need of seeing, and how beneficial is it that we in Christian ministries clothe ourselves in the manner Paul describes when ministering to individuals or families in other or similar situations?

Case Study: Sally and Joseph's Family Crisis

◘"I'm the one to blame! I'm to blame!" That is the sad refrain Sally kept repeating throughout the days leading up to the funeral of her seventeen year old son. Joey died shortly after falling into a drug-induced coma. The cause of death, according to the doctors, was related to complications associated with the combination of several illicit drugs and a fatal overdose. Since the overdose, Sally has taken to blaming herself and nothing either her pastor or husband Joseph has said has seemed to convince her otherwise. "I'm to blame," is all she kept saying as she rocked back and forth in a chair in Joey's room. Sally refuses to leave the room. Her appearance is that of a broken woman. "Her spirit is completely broken," the pastor reports to his pastoral care staff. "All the light seems drained from her eyes. She's not eating or drinking regularly and has not slept for more than a couple of hours for days."

Even though Sally had been serving in her local church and has professed Christ as her savior for most of her adult life, it is as if nothing in scripture could console her grief. She has expressed to her husband, Joseph, who hardly attends church, that God has abandoned her and that whatever happened to destroy her son's life had to be her fault. Joseph is becoming increasingly more worried about his wife's condition—so much so that he has arranged for his sister to stay by her side whenever he leaves the house. He has never really been a big believer in God or had any appreciation for going to church, but he certainly is not blaming his son's death on any god. In trying to cope with his own loss and grief the thing most pressing for him, aside from his wife's state of mind, is his two other children, nineteen-year-old Sara, who suffers periodically from an anxiety disorder and seven-year-old John, who suffers from severe learning disabilities and is in need of special attention to complete school work. Little John, as he is called, is the main catalyst for the pastor's visit to see the family that day. One Sunday after church, John was crying as he told the children's pastor that he did not want to go home because everyone there was too unhappy and sad.

The children's pastor brought the issue to the attention of the senior pastor who was already familiar with the situation and visited with the family and Joey in the hospital before Joey died. As the two pastors discussed the matter, they acknowledged that the family is in crisis with unknown ramifications. Unfortunately, there is no one on the pastoral staff trained to deal with the complex nature of the psychological issues that are overlapping with the spiritual concerns. They know all too well that in times like these it's important to pray and seek guidance, but prayer alone will not be enough. This family needs immediate interventions and multifaceted services to address the spiritual, psychological and social issues. "What can we do?" the children's pastor wondered out loud. "Do we just wait and see if the family is able to find help? Are these needs beyond the scope of pastoral care?"

Theological Reflections: Serving Others in Their Time of Trouble

"Over all these virtues put on love and servanthood."
Colossians 3:13

When pastors and other ministers find themselves in the middle of situations such as that described in the case study above, they naturally will wonder where in the community families in crisis might be able to turn for help. In fact, most people get into ministry to come alongside people who are in need and to help them. However, the reality is that Christian leadership and ministry is not always as simple as that. Along the way, we have come to realize that in serving others, there are often competing voices concerning a myriad of needs that vie for our attention. Though those voices are not always evil or wrong, at times they can be distracting and misleading. As conscientious church leaders, we continually have to revisit biblical teachings, in particular Jesus' teachings, to shape and refresh our understanding of ministry and leadership and in order to help those we serve. The case concerning Sally and her family really challenges us to get back to two basic theological building blocks: love and servanthood. One of the greatest gospel texts that direct us to this conclusion is the conversation between Jesus and a man considered as an expert in the Law. The story is recorded in Luke chapter 10. The man in that story came to Jesus, seeking to engage Him in a conversation about good deeds that are necessary to gain eternal life. He asked Jesus, *"What must I do to inherit eternal life?"* Jesus responded by asking the man to interpret certain portions of the Law that outlines how to live in relation to God and his fellowman.

The man quoted from the Law, saying, "Love the Lord your God with all your heart and with all your soul and with all your strength and with all your mind'; and, *Love your neighbor as yourself*."[3] Jesus affirms the man's answer, but then the man asked Jesus for clarification as to who are the people God expects him to love: *"Who is my neighbor?"* Instead of giving some kind of an abstract response, Jesus chose to present a concrete case study using a parable related to a man from a people group known then as enemies to Israelites, such as the man with whom Jesus spoke. Jesus referred to the actions of a single Samaritan man towards his neighbor. Jesus described an encounter between a Samaritan and another Middle-Eastern man whom he found possibly dying on the side of a road. The man was a victim of a brutal crime perpetrated upon him in a very bad neighborhood. In that well-known parable, the victim was found severely beaten, robbed and then left at the side of a road to die. Not much information was provided about the victim except that he was in need of all sorts of assistance. However, Jesus goes on to tell of two Jewish religious leaders who passed by and saw the man but failed to provide any help.

Reading the story of the Samaritan, one might think it could have been that the religious leaders were in a hurry or that they were too distracted by other religious duties to see that the beaten man needed their help; or maybe they thought that helping this man was not their responsibility. Through their lack of action, Jesus illustrates that the religious leaders were not clothed with love. As Christian leaders, we too can often find ourselves with numerous excuses for not helping those in need, conscious or unconscious. It is so easy for our calendars and busy schedules to control and dictate our actions. Many of us find ourselves slow to respond to those in need because of thoughts like: "Is this a legitimate need? I'm not equipped to solve these persons' problem, they got themselves into the jam," or "Someone else will help them." These thoughts can directly shape our responses. In contrast to the religious leaders, the Samaritan man stopped and provided the beaten victim with tangible help, social services if you will. The Samaritan administered first aid, provided transportation and lodging during the victim's incapacitation, and then took financial responsibility, seeing to it that the man was cared for during his recovery from the ordeal.[4] The story indicates that the Samaritan responded to a victim of crime even outside his own community. The question often asked concerning the Samaritan man is, "Why would he stop and help this man?" Jesus says that when the Samaritan saw the beaten man, he was moved by compassion.[5]

In our case study concerning Sally and her family, we too have presented people who are in crisis, just like the beaten man at the side of the road in the Samaritan narrative. Our aim is to consider the roles of the two pastors involved and the role of the church in coming to the aid of the family. Like the Samaritan, they could help to the best of their ability and training but it might also be necessary to consult or solicit the help of others (as the Samaritan did with the innkeeper) with expertise in assessing the family's needs and providing some interventions. This also is where the roles of social workers and other skilled professionals come into the picture. We will have an opportunity in the upcoming section, entitled "Reality Dialogue", to explore more about the value of developing such collaborative relationships for ministry. In ministry, the call to love others and to servanthood is not a call to independence in ministry but greater dependence on God and fellow servants as is clearly demonstrated in the parable of the Samaritan.

In the text, Jesus asserts that loving God is the first and greatest commandment and the highest priority. Nothing has changed. Love for God remains es-

sentially the motivating force in our ministries. Further, Jesus teaches us that
tied closely and related to the commandment of loving God is the divine command to love others. Our love for God is to overflow into our love for others, no
matter their gender, race, or socio-economic condition. Matthew Henry puts it
this way: "It is the duty of every one of us, in our places, and according to our
ability, to succor, help, and relieve all that is in distress and need."[6]

Jesus teaches that love of others is depicted best in a life lived towards servanthood. In fact, servanthood is often understood as Godly love demonstrated
with humans' hands and feet. Similar to compassion, servanthood is love in action. The Samaritan man, moved by compassion, demonstrated servanthood by
putting the needs of the wounded man before his personal needs, interests and
affairs. Jesus says, *"If anyone wants to be first, he must be the very last, and the
servant of all."*[7] He has turned the understanding of leadership upside down.
Robert Greenleaf, who popularized servant leadership in the 1970s, in essence
paraphrases Jesus' words when he writes, "The great leader is seen as servant
first."[8] Servanthood strives "to make sure that other people's highest priority
needs are being served."[9]

Jesus was not just talking about servant actions. He also desired servanthood to be a virtue of his followers. J. Oswald Sanders suggests, "Jesus' teaching on servanthood and suffering was not intended merely to inspire good behavior. Jesus wanted to impart the spirit of servanthood, the sense of personal
commitment and identity that He expressed when He said, 'I am among you as
one who serves."[10] Even Jesus' personal mission statement exemplifies servanthood. Jesus said of himself, "The Spirit of the Lord is on me, because he has
anointed me to preach good news to the poor. He has sent me to proclaim freedom for the prisoners and recovery of sight for the blind, to release the oppressed, to proclaim the year of the Lord's favor."[11] This inaugural statement of
his ministry solidly connects Jesus' mission to serving hopeless and broken
people. Jesus' restorative ministry adds to our understanding of servant leadership.

Let us begin now to focus more closely on the details of the case study on
Sally and Joseph's Family Crisis. Each member of the family appears to be in
need of some form of restorative care and love. At first glance, Sally and her
children might be seen as the ones who most deserve to receive pastoral care and
assistance; after all, they have been attending the church. Some might say, "If
Sally, who is the adult Christian in the home, is not healthy and whole, how can
the rest of the family experience the healing made available in Christ?" However, we find no biblical foundation for such a view. In the scriptures servant leadership and restorative actions are not limited by age, gender or spiritual journey. Moreover, when viewing from a more systemic perspective, we see that the
whole family needs to encounter Christians who are clothed in the virtues that
Paul wrote about (love, compassion, kindness, humility, gentleness patience,
etc.). The pastors in the case study have a unique opportunity to help Sally's
family as they bear each other's burdens, forgive one another and strive to over-

come their trials. With the pastors' help, the family can be closely bound together in unity and love as they move through their time of crisis.

The Apostle Paul speaks of Christians' sacrificial service to others and a willingness to suffer hardship for the sake of the Gospel.[12] As Jesus illustrated in the Samaritan parable, Godly love and servant-like actions should be extended to people who are part of the community of Christ as well as those not yet a part of the Christian community. Paul challenges Christian leaders to extend their helping hands beyond the wall of the church, to those who are not yet followers of Christ. In the case study, for example, Joseph is not to be excluded from pastoral care simply because he does not attend the church. Clearly, Paul embraced Jesus' teachings on servanthood as he passed the teachings on to all of the followers of Christ. When addressing freedom in Christ, Paul conveyed that, a most important aspect of the Christian belief is to know that Godly faith is always expressed through love.[13] He goes on to show that our freedom in Christ is not for selfish gains but for serving one another.[14]

Though love and servanthood are addressed time and time again in ministry settings, we all need a little refocusing along the way. The Samaritan man in the parable of Jesus and Paul's letter to the church in Colossae remind Christian leaders of the basics of Jesus' ministry to the hopeless and broken. Each challenges us to remember not to overlook people around us as we attend to our own priorities and interests. Over all the many virtues and skills required for ministry, we as the church are to clothe ourselves with love and servanthood so those in our society might see and recognize God in us.

Connecting Pastoral Care and Social Work Practice

Using the case study, we are able to identify some of the main concerns that naturally emerge as we discuss each individual, the entire family and the role of the church. Our interest in this case centers on finding a proper balance between meeting the social and psychological needs without losing sight of our primary role of communicating the gospel. Although very few details were provided in the case concerning the pastors' role, it is importance to recognize their desire to look to other professionals and even the community for resources. Their goal was to address comprehensively the crisis and the ongoing needs of the family. Ministries of helping, such as pastoral care or social work, share a long and rich religious history. We will rely on those respective traditions and values to show some of the most efficacious ways to go about responding to families within and around our communities.

For instance, in one of the best book available on church social work, entitled *Church Social Work: Helping the whole person in the context of the church*, the editor, Diana Garland, states that "unlike professional social work in the broader community agency setting, the church social worker has as a primary task the responsibility of equipping people in ministry to serve."[15] It is important for those of us in ministry to be able to recognize when it is necessary to consult professionals, trained in the art and science of assessing, evaluating, and counseling individuals and families, as is the case with Sally and her family. The case study highlights several opportunities for consultation to help each family member and the family as a whole. We will discuss each matter further in the upcoming section that is entitled, "Reality Dialogue Questions," For now; let us consider the role that a social worker might play in the church in general and then specifically the case study. Garland describes the role of church social workers as follows:

> Church social workers bring the social work profession's knowledge, values, and skills to the church as a resource. They help the church understand the needs of persons, define those needs and a ministry challenge central to the mission of the church, and equip church members for effective service and/or social action. For example, in response to the problems of homelessness in a church community, a church social worker educates the church about the complex of factors that create homelessness. The social worker guides the church in a study of response of the people of God to homelessness in the Bible and in the history of the church, and a study of the theological ramification of responses the church can take. Finally, if the church decides to involve itself, the social worker helps the church develop programs of ministry to homeless persons and actions for speaking out on the issues that place persons and families at risk for homelessness.[16]

After considering the questions below and reading the "Synergistic Dialogue" that follows, readers should develop some thoughts concerning the benefits of forming collaborations between pastoral care ministers and church social workers to minister effectively to hurting individuals and families. Each minister is trained in his or her respective field, yet both rely on the same Biblical foundation in order to find the necessary balance to minister to the spiritual and temporal needs of hurting people. Finally, as each question is addressed we get a sense of the naturalness of the trust and respect that is exemplified in such collaborations between pastoral care ministry and church social work.

Reality Dialogue Questions

Should the pastors take Sally's family crisis as an opportunity to engage with that family and other professionals in the community? How might those in church social work respond to this family during and after the crisis?

Most definitely, we have learned from Jesus' teachings and even Paul's letter showing that each encounter with people in need should be viewed as a divine opportunity to impart the virtues of God. Sally's family presents a great opportunity for the church to help them as they bear through the pains of the crisis and to connect with social service delivery systems within the broader community. The family is experiencing profound loss and grief on very personal levels, and specific social problems related to epidemics of drug abuse, suicide and mental illness in our society. Such a family would need to rely on all of their internal resources as well as some from the outside in order to survive the tragedy of the loss of their family member, loss of health and wellbeing. Too often opportunities are missed in our fast-paced world when we do not stop to pay close attention to the cares of those around us. Truly the lessons of the Samaritan story is befitting to this family and the two pastors from the local church. Yet another story might also come to mind; the one indicated in John 9, wherein a man who was blind from birth encounters Jesus and he healed him. "As he [*Jesus*] went along . . . His disciples asked him, 'Rabbi, who sinned, this man or his parents, that he was born blind?' 'Neither this man nor his parents sinned,' said Jesus, 'but this happened so that the work of God might be displayed in his life. As long as it is day, we must do the work of him who sent me. Night is coming, when no one can work." Jesus spoke of the problem as an opportunity for God's grace to be manifested to the man, his family and the entire community. At no point in the story was the man's status in the synagogue raised. As pastors and ministers, we are granted special opportunities to reflect Christ's hands and heart extended to the world around us. Moreover, as we read the story in John 9, we discovered that Jesus made a couple of referrals after healing the blind man. For instance, he sent him to carry out a cultural rite of washing himself... "Wash in the Pool of Siloam." His community then presented him to the local leaders to discuss the miracle which he and his family experienced. It was by seizing the opportunity to help the blind man and his family that others in the community learned about Jesus' work and God's grace; might it be the same with us.

Do you know that the profession of social work owes much of its origin to Judeo-Christian teachings? Oh, yes, it does. In fact, the Professional Values of the social work profession remains deeply rooted in Christian principles. As mentioned earlier, church social workers have a role to play in equipping people in ministry to serve. In the case study, the role of social workers becomes evident when we realize that it is important for the two pastors to recognize that it is necessary to find out whether Sally's family have been referred for proper consultations with professionals trained in assessing, evaluating, and counseling individuals and families with problems. It is quite possible that the family is already in connection with some sort of social service agencies within the community, possibly through the social work department in the hospital where the son, Joey, died. However, one should not assume that the family is receiving such services; it is important to ask whether their needs are being addressed. Assisted by social workers, a minister who might be the first person to engage with the family is in a key position to ensure linkages between the family and social services that are available in the community. Church leaders will learn more about the strengths and limitations of social services that are available in their local community, when they further engage with people who are in need of such services. As more churches begin to work closely with local and church social workers, they will find increased opportunities to be involved in helping to design and develop outreach programs for people in need and even present their voice at the table among groups seeking to address families such as Sally's that are at risk for drug abuse and suicide.

Synergistic Dialogue: Fruit of the Spirit and Professional Competency

"I waited while you spoke.
I listened to your reasoning"
Job 32:10-11

In this section, as in most subsequent chapters we, Doctors Grenz and Albertini, engage readers in a series of conversation that we call "Synergistic Dialogues." Each set of dialogue presents our views on a respective case study. Dr. Grenz's role in the conversation is to bring out a pastoral viewpoint while Dr. Albertini's role is to offer a social worker's viewpoint. In this chapter's dialogue, Dr. Grenz starts the conversation concerning the case study on *Sally and Joseph's Family Crisis.*

Grenz
As I approach the case study, I find myself initially being quite introspective. What would I bring to this crisis? I somehow feel ill-equipped to be of help and I believe that many pastors have similar feelings. It seems that when we feel ill-equipped we are fearful of fully engaging people in need and there is a tendency to want to avoid it. It is easy to simply pray with the family, walk away and wait for them to call with a specific need.

Albertini
In reading the case study, I agree that it does require some introspection. I could see where someone without a background in counseling or social work might become overwhelmed and might be tempted to avoid becoming fully involved. The family's situation was very complex. However, the case study highlights two main areas for development that involves both the pastoral team and social service providers. For instance, in an effort to respond to Sally's family, there are two key areas of focus: 1) the need to link the family with social services as soon as possible to assess and address the personal and family needs;

and 2) the need to provide support related to spiritual dimensions. Here we find that the entire family is grieving and no doubt planning for a funeral for Joey. Perhaps the best way to approach these two key areas is to identify a few key questions that the pastoral team, I am sure, will need to answer, such as, How are they doing? What do they need? In addition, how might the church help?

G renz
As I hear your questions, I'm reminded of much of my own pastoral care training. If this family does not have the extended family supports and social service networks established, it might be more difficult for them to cope and survive. However, it would be an ideal opportunity for the church to help them to begin to develop their network. I see how the church would need to reach out to Joseph and the rest of the family with pastoral care. I also wonder how the church might represent God to Joseph. It is possible that Joseph has had a bad experience with churches. Though prayer is a powerful tool which God has given us, we too often only offer prayer as our service to people. I could see myself in a conversation with Joseph where I would naturally say, If you like, "Joseph, we will pray for you, Sally and your children." However, for many unchurched individuals who are skeptical of the church, this is not enough for a breakthrough. The fruit of the Spirit that indwells followers of Christ needs to be seen in practical, tangible ways. From a pastor's viewpoint, Joseph ultimately needs Jesus in his life, but like Jesus, who often started with a person's physical or social needs, pastors and their staff needs to embody that approach.

A lbertini
I would like to know more about your perspective as a pastor and I will share my views as well.

G renz
Well, from a pastoral care perspective, first I would say it needs to be a team effort. A community of loving followers of Christ needs to engage this family. For example, the children's pastor or an *appropriate* children's ministry volunteer could reach out to help John (the seven-year-old with learning disabilities) get some tutoring. Of course, this person would need Joseph's permission. I hope that because the church offers tangible help that Joseph would grant permission. Another aspect of this help is that it is grounded in relationship and community. It is likely that Joseph will need to trust the church members if he is going to allow them to serve his family.

A lbertini
I agree that showing love and building trust is a good place to begin with the family. The spiritual, psychological and social dimensions of the situation for each family member are important aspects of the problems as well as the solutions that this family and those offering help will need to consider. As a church social worker, I would want to know that Joseph and Sally are aware that

first and foremost the representatives of the church are there to offer spiritual as well as tangible support to help in dealing with the crisis. This family is facing tremendous loss and grief. The social work approach would involve very clear and purposeful steps taken toward helping each individual in the family to identify and deal with problems he or she faces. When appropriate, the social worker's aim is to link people with other people and places that provide individual and family assessments, carefully designed plans for interventions, counseling throughout the process of recovery and ongoing evaluation and progress updates. That might include for this family immediate help, if they accept it, in the form of crisis intervention. The social workers' role spans a variety of specialized areas—medical social work, school social work and clinical social work, just to name a few.

G renz

One of the key roles for the church staff is to identify and assess the available resources in the community that would help Joseph and his family. One thing that I have found is that most pastors tend to focus only on Christian community services, like a Christian counselor. I don't think that there is anything wrong with connecting with Christian counselors in the community. However, I believe that many times we miss out on other great services (and often inexpensive) that are available in the community. I learned this from my Care Ministry Coordinator in my last church. I employed someone at our church who was a social worker by profession. She connected people with free services like grief support groups and counseling. My big question is, How do you assess such service providers to make sure they will be helpful and that they are not promoting ideas that theologically disagree with Biblical teachings?

A lbertini

You have raised a very good point; not all social service providers are the same in terms of their theological or philosophical worldview. The key is to be able to determine who, offers the most effective social services, and to be certain that individuals and families you refer are matched with the appropriate help they need. It is important to consider the person's religious background. This might seem too simple an idea but it is possible for church leaders and other ministers to call and speak with service providers to determine whether the quality and type of services they provide should be included in the church's listing of social services. A good question to ask service providers, for example, is whether their philosophical approaches are compatible with the beliefs of people in the Christian community. It would be a matter of adding and removing some providers from the churches' list of service providers. The point is not to be afraid to ask important questions of the service providers in the community. Like other businesses and non-profit organizations, social service providers might be willing to hire workers who are able to address the needs of large numbers of people referred from local churches. Remember the saying, "*We have not because we ask not.*" Churches do not all have to look the same in terms of how their network of resources are organized; some churches might already have social workers on staff while other might develop extensive working relationships with social workers in the local community. Many Christians who possess the social work degree are employed in local agencies; they are untapped resources in churches.

Conclusion

People expect that those who deliver the gospel are capable of bringing truth and comfort to those around them. In preparing preachers to preach, God uses them as agents of care and change, not only in churches but in broader communities. Thus, pastoral care includes ministries that actively engage people who are in need, and when appropriate, it might call for the assessment of numerous personal and social issues that affect people's lives. Sometimes pastors who attempt to extend care to people who are in need of social services might find themselves venturing beyond their ministerial training and skills. In such cases, it is necessary for pastors to work with other skilled professionals in order to connect people with social services in agencies throughout their community. Developing and working with networks of non-clergy professionals requires time, effort, and wisdom, but by doing so, pastors will discover many helpful partners in their communities. For instance, Sally's family experiences with local pastors in her community, as described in the case study, provide insights into the benefits of collaborations between pastors, social workers and other professionals.

In the upcoming chapter, there is an opportunity to explore other pressing issues facing church leaders—especially those in urban communities. The discussion concerns people who are experiencing homelessness and some ancillary personal and social problems—drug dependence and abuse. Such issues merit inclusion in our discourse on the collaborative approach to ministry.   Readers might recall that in the preface of this book, the discussion of synergistic collaborations between pastors and social workers began with two basic questions. We asked whether, as part of the American church, we are finding ourselves in more of a proactive or reactive posture in relation to all the socioeconomic and political changes that are taking place. By now, readers might have surmised that Christ has fully equipped the church with all that is needed to fulfill the Great Commission. Yet, some church leaders might be less prepared than others to monitor the cultural changes that are taking place and to respond in ways that meet the new challenges. Nonetheless, Christ remains sovereign and therefore the perfection of his work will be fulfilled.

CHAPTER 2

When Homeless People in the Community Come Knocking, Do I Let Them In?

Introduction: Where is the church?

Imagine if you would, that it was possible for you to inquire of all human beings, both past and present, about the location of the sun. What might their responses be? You might agree that no matter to whom, or when you pose the question, that the location will have to be the same. Everyone answering such a question, barring of course some debilitating mental impairment, would have to indicate that the sun is up in the sky. In fact, for us, the sun has only ever existed there. Regardless of culture or geographic location, people will point upward to locate the sun. Similarly, if it were possible to inquire about places where worship occurs, most likely people would single out their sacred places of worship.

People are able to locate places of worship because, as anthropology confirms, all people groups on earth practice some form of religion in specific places.[1] However, if instead of asking about the location of the sun or places of worship, you were to inquire about the "Church of Jesus Christ," then the answers might vary significantly. In fact, some people might point to cathedrals and other structures built specifically for Christian worship, and in so doing provide descriptions of Christian churches. Others might quote Scriptures that use analogies such as "bride of Christ" or "body of Christ" to describe the church. With such analogy, they would of course be referring specifically to followers of Christ, associating the followers' beliefs and practices with the united global Christian community. People serving in Christian ministries might even elaborate further to identify people whom they serve as members of the church. Working within the premise that American churches are being afforded new opportunities to teach about the life and work of Christ, one should remember that it is important to explore fully the location and role of the church of Jesus Christ as described in Scripture. In doing so, we will develop a better understanding of effective ways for churches to serve people of our time.

By exploring the richness of the role of churches in society as described in Scripture, we will arrive at a unified concept of the church. Only then will we be able to allay concerns over whether American churches are called to employ a reactive rather than a proactive response to changes that are taking place around us. The exploration will also allow us to decipher whether American churches and church leaders should attempt to grasp the implications of how certain social changes might influence the ways in which we do ministry. It is important to understand the implications, especially of socioeconomic and political changes that are influencing the church's role in fulfilling the Great Commission.[2] As we begin the exploration, let us focus our attention on the following case study that involves a conversation between a seasoned pastor, James Broen, and one of his mentees, Phillip Starr.

In the case study, Starr is a young pastor who is newly appointed to a small inner-city church. The conversation between the two pastors centers on challenges which Starr's church is facing as he and the congregation confront two of the most challenging social issues of the inner city, homelessness, and drug and alcohol addictions. The church as discussed earlier is finding that an increasing number of people are turning to non-government organizations such as churches and parachurch organizations for help.[3]

Case Study: So much homelessness—what are pastors to do?

◼Pastors Broen and Starr met for their first of a year-long series of mentoring sessions. The two gentlemen agreed to meet at a local restaurant near the church where Pastor Broen had been serving for over ten years. The mentoring sessions provide opportunities for the new pastor to learn the ropes, so to speak, as they talk about how to address the spiritual and social needs of the people within the church and community. After an opening prayer, Pastor Broen commented that he would be available to discuss all issues that Pastor Starr felt were challenging, either in ministry or his personal life. He also informed Pastor Starr that he was responsible for mentoring several other new pastors in his denomination. In Starr's case, the mentoring relationship developed with great ease; this was partly because he grew up as a teenager in a church where Broen's older brother served as the senior pastor. Having already met Pastor Broen, he was able to open up quite quickly about his experiences.

Over lunch, Broen began by asking Starr whether there were any issues related to ministry that Starr found particularly challenging. In response, Starr shared some of his concerns about the physical location of his church, identifying it as one of the poorest areas in the inner-city. Starr further explained how on a daily basis he and his staff confront the local problem of homelessness and alcoholism. He said that they have to lock the doors of the church in order to deter homeless people, especially those who are drunk, from simply wandering in off the streets.

"What do you mean?" Broen asked in a prompting tone.

Starr: I mean that we have to lock the church's doors during the day. If not, we would not be able to deal with the number of people who try to get into the church to ask for help and some form of social services. They come for everything from food, to a place to bathe, to money. At first, we thought we could handle it and so we tried to help, but they just kept coming in increasing numbers. Like many churches, we have a small amount of money set aside for benevolent funds used primarily to help people in our congregation who find themselves in crisis; however, it is nowhere near enough to help those who wander in off the streets and from all around the community. Moreover, with our long-term plan of developing a pre-school, we do not want to develop the sort of reputation that encourages large numbers of homeless people to hang around the grounds, if you know what I mean.

Broen: It seems that this has been weighing heavily on your mind.

Starr: It has. Well, take yesterday, for example; I had to chase—literally chase—an elderly woman off the property. She's what we call a repeat offender. She keeps coming by to use a garden hose we used to leave outside. She comes by to wash her hair and sometimes her clothes. Most of the times that woman is drunk or high. A few times, we did give her a few bucks to go and get something to eat. Each time she would just stagger away. Lately, I decided to have the garden hose locked away in hopes of dissuading her from coming onto the property. Now get this! Last Tuesday we found a homeless man sleeping under a church bus parked on our lot. Just think about it. The driver could easily have run him over. The homeless people we see present some safety issues. Sometimes we have to get the police involved and have them removed from the property, with hopes that they will not return.

Broen: Sounds like you have had some very difficult situations to deal with. If you were to identify the main challenge your church faces, what would you say that it is?

Starr: The main problem doesn't have as much to do with us having to chase the drunks and homeless people away on a daily basis; given our location that has to be expected. We knew we would have some of that problem when we bought the property at such a low price, in the heart of the inner-city. The issue isn't the people; it is deciding just how much of the social problems we are to take on. I also have trouble sleeping at nights just dealing with the feelings of not having done enough at the end of the day. I know that there is just so much that a small church can do. Yet, I come away each day with a nagging feeling about each homeless or alcohol-addicted person we chased off. I often think of Jesus' words concerning the poor and the sick...you know... "I tell you the truth, whatever you did not do for one of the least, of these you did not do for me."4 Some days the staff and I even wonder, did we just turn Jesus away?

Theological Reflections: Tattered and Worn

"Over all these virtues show love and mercy"
I Timothy 1:6

How should Christ's followers respond to issues of homelessness, alcoholism and even poverty in general? How should churches respond to the poor who are right outside their doors? For this theological reflection, our focus will first be on poverty, because many people who struggle with poverty are at risk for experiencing homelessness, unstable housing, and substance abuse issues.[5] Initially, some Christians, especially Westerners, might say that when it comes to people who are enthralled in conditions of poverty, it is best to respond less charitably, viewing poverty as a direct result of poor decisions or laziness on the part of those in poverty. After all, charity to such would only cultivate dependency. Some Christians might want to ignore or avoid those in poverty because they view work with the poor as dirty, unpleasant, and difficult.

Before addressing a biblical understanding of poverty, we must explore two foundational biblical concepts. The first of these is the sanctity of life. This idea is often associated with the issue of abortion; however, it extends beyond that issue. It relates to the value of all within humanity. Sanctity of life can be defined as:

> The conviction that all human beings, in any and every state of consciousness or self-awareness, of any and every race, color, ethnicity, level of intelligence, religion, language, nationality, gender, character, behavior, physical ability/disability, potential, class, social status, etc., of any and every particular quality of relationship to the viewing subject, are to be perceived as sacred, as persons of equal and immeasurable worth and of inviolable dignity. Therefore, they must be treated with the reverence and respect commensurate with this elevated moral status.[6]

The sanctity of life is grounded in the creation narrative in Genesis 1:

> And God said, "Let us make man in our image, in our likeness, and let them rule over the fish of the sea and the birds of the air, over the livestock, over all the earth, and over all the creatures that move along the ground." So God created man in his own image, in the image of God he created him; male and female he created them. (Genesis 1:26-27)

Each person's value resides in the fact that we are all created in God's image. This concept is also strengthened in Jesus' teaching in Matthew 25:31-46. Jesus challenges each of us to see him in the face of each person, no matter the gender, ethnicity, nationality, social status, or even behavior.

The second foundational biblical concept we need to address before looking specifically at the issue of poverty is the concept of forgiveness. Often forgiveness is related to our relationship with God or with those who have hurt us. Yet, forgiveness extends beyond these ideas. Jesus' interaction with the woman caught in adultery in John 8 challenges us to expand not just our understanding of forgiveness, but also our application of forgiveness. How was Jesus able to minister to this woman? The answer to this question is found in verse 11. After Jesus asked the woman where her accusers were, Jesus said to her, "Then neither do I condemn you ...go and leave your life of sin" (Jn 8:11). Jesus was able to forgive her for her sinful lifestyle. Though we are not Jesus, and do not, have the authority to absolve someone of his or her sins, we do have the ability to forgive him or her for mistakes made, so we are able to see him or her free of our condemnation. Forgiveness frees us to reach out to others and minister to them in their hurt. Beyond these two foundational biblical concepts, the Bible informs us of God's view of poverty and challenges followers of Christ to respond to this issue. First, let's explore God's view of poverty.

The words "poor" (the physical nature) and "poverty" appear around 300 times in the Bible.[7] Ronald J. Sider, author of *Just Generosity: A new vision for overcoming poverty in America,* did a great job in synthesizing these biblical texts into four points. The first point is that the Bible repeatedly states that God lifts up the poor and oppressed (Ex 3:7-8; 6:5-7; Dt 26:6-8; Ps 12:5). For example, the psalmist wrote, "My whole being will exclaim, 'Who is like you, O LORD?'" You rescue the poor from those too strong for them, the poor and needy from those who rob them.'" (Ps 35:10). The second point is that sometimes God tears down rich and powerful people because of their treatment of the poor (Ps 10; Isa 3:14-25; Jer 22:13-19; Am 5:11-12; 6:4; Jas 5:2-6). The reality is that some wealthy people get wealthy by oppressing or mistreating the poor or some neglect the needs of the poor, similar to Mr. Scrooge from *The Christmas Carol.* The prophet Jeremiah communicated this very clearly when he wrote:

> "Among my people are wicked men who lie in wait like men who snare birds and like those who set traps to catch men. Like cages full of birds, their houses are full of deceit; they have become rich and powerful and have grown fat and

sleek. Their evil deeds have no limit; they do not plead the case of the fatherless to win it, they do not defend the rights of the poor. Should I not punish them for this?" declares the LORD. "Should I not avenge myself on such a nation as this?" (Jer 5:26-29)

The Bible does not have a negative view of wealth, but does chastise those who forget to share their wealth. Sider's third point is that God identifies with the poor so strongly that caring for them is almost like helping God. Jesus' parable of the sheep and the goats in Matthew 25 emphasizes this point: "Whatever you did for the one of the least of these brothers of mine, you did for me" (Mt 25:40). Some scholars suggest that this parable is a commentary of some Old Testament texts. One such text is Proverbs 19:17, "He who is kind to the poor lends to the Lord." The last point is that God calls his children to treat the poor in the same way he has treated them (Ex 22:21-24; Dt 15:13-15). Just think about Paul's words in 2 Corinthians 8:9, "For you know the grace of our Lord Jesus Christ, that though he was rich, yet for your sakes he became poor, so that you through his poverty might become rich." God even goes so far as to insist that if we do not imitate God's concern for the poor, we are not really his people (also see Is 58:3-7; Jer 22:13-19; Am 5:21-24; 1 Jn 3:17). Going back to Jesus' parable in Matthew 25, those who thought they were going to heaven but failed to feed the hungry were condemned (Mt 25:45-46).[8]

The mission of the church is also critical to the discussion. Adverse reactions to the "Social Gospel" movement of the nineteenth century have caused many to ignore the church's social responsibility and hold evangelism as its primary mandate. Yet, how can the church ignore the biblical foundation we just addressed? The question becomes: What is the relationship between evangelism and social responsibility? One possible way to answer this is to understand mission as "everything the church is sent into the world to do."[9] This would include not only evangelism, but also social action. Along with the gospel message coming out of our mouths, our reaching arms and hands, need to extend to those suffering in poverty. When referring to Jesus' earthly ministry, Charles Colson states, "He [Jesus] was concerned not only with saving man from hell in the next world, but with delivering him from the hellishness of this one."[10] The early church also emphasized social responsibility. "The Christian community offered an array of social services too. Christians cared for widows and orphans, visited prisoners, fed the poor, nursed the sick, and buried the dead. Church members gave freely of their money to support these various ministries."[11]

It seems that many churches have lost sight of how God views poverty and the fuller understanding of their mission as a church. As God's ambassadors here on earth, we must open our eyes and hearts to those struggling in poverty, and extend our arms and hands in gracious, providing ways.

Reality Dialogue Question

How long should Christians or churches as a whole reach out to people who are homeless or addicted to alcohol or other substances?

Serving persons who are homeless and those caught up in the vicious cycle of addictions to alcohol or other mind-altering substances is one of the most challenging areas of ministry. It is difficult for families, churches and social service agencies to find effective ways of helping such people to escape the social and spiritual traps of such problems. Yet, those are the very areas of ministry that neither society nor the church can afford to abandon. Such areas of ministry just do not fit within the norms of traditional Sunday morning services. Sunday morning is usually the time Christians set aside to collectively express their worship to God and observe other traditions set forth in the Scriptures. Although such services often include prayers for the sick and the downcast, the services are not structured in ways to address directly the individual's struggle with homelessness or alcoholism. Even though some pastors' sermons might include teachings on the personal, spiritual and social nature of homelessness or alcoholism, the complexities of the issues require a more direct approach than is usually available in a Sunday morning sermon.

The question remains: How long should Christians or churches as a whole reach out to people who are homeless or addicted to alcohol or other substances? Perhaps instead of focusing on the quantity of time and aid, we should be focusing on the quality of time and aid needed to address the needs of the homeless and addicted persons. In addition, it might make a difference in developing our views if we were to focus our attention not so much on the amount of time in service or ministry that is needed but rather on the quality of ministry. We might even ask ourselves, What if we were in that situation? How you or I would want to be treated? What if it was a family member? Imagine that the homeless person we are talking about was actually one of your own sons or daughters, parents or close friends. Would a relative as opposed to a stranger, being in the situation, make it easier to envision the need to focus on the quality of services to be provided as opposed to quantity to be spent providing aid?

Synergistic Dialogue: A Mile in Their Shoes

"Taking good care of strangers, you could be
entertaining angels without knowing it. "
Hebrew 13:2

A lbertini
I tell you the truth; if ever I were to find myself homeless or struggling with an addiction, I would hope that someone or some group would do all that they could to help me to escape my plight. The Scripture that comes to mind for me is, "So in everything, do to others what you would have them do to you for this sums up the Law and the Prophets."[12] The thought of never giving up on a fellow human being also comes to the forefront of my mind. For some it might take weeks, or months, while for others it might take years for them to overcome such challenges. I say that as long as someone continues to bear the image of God and despite his or her condition in life, he or she is worth our best effort. The Scripture describes some personal and spiritual problems as strongholds. The term "stronghold" indicates that there are no easy fixes for individuals struggling with strongholds or for those who might be reaching out to help them. The Scripture also speaks of the need to offer grace continually and forgiveness completely to others.[13]

G renz
Paul mentions strongholds in 2 Corinthians 10:4-5. These strongholds are the thoughts, arguments, plans and everything that opposes itself to Christ. For many who are struggling with addictions and other issues, they are bound by the thoughts and arguments that Satan (an adversary) has convinced them to be true. Paul taught that some strongholds cannot be demolished by our own strength. Only by the power of God through the blood of Jesus Christ can some strong-holds be destroyed. It seems then that one's spiritual condition, as well as, one's physical, social and economic condition needs to change for him or her to expe-rience true freedom.

A lbertini
You are so correct in associating strongholds with the lack of freedom. So often, when people are struggling to be free from conditions of homelessness or alcoholism, their family and friends give up on them in frustration or forsake them in order to preserve the rest of the family. It is difficult to find ongoing resources to offer sustained aid. Often there are feelings of disappointment, fru-stration, pain, and anger associated with the circumstances. Therefore, there is the need to discuss forgiveness. It was Peter in the Scriptures who once went up to Christ and asked him, "Lord, how often will my brother sin against me, and I forgive him. . . . As many as seven times? Jesus said to him, "I do not say to you

seven times, but seventy times seven. The aim is to reach for perfection in our efforts, as indicated by the phrase, seventy times seven.[14] In other words, keep offering *appropriate* aid until it works. As a social worker, I subscribe to the belief that everyone should be afforded service as needed. It is a part of our profession's Core Values. Services might take many forms. In the case of individuals who are homeless or addicted to substances, it will take specialized skills and training to provide the necessary psycho-social-spiritual assessments, interventions, and case management to address comprehensively their short and long term rehabilitative needs.

G renz
This is where many churches and church leaders become overwhelmed. Traditionally, most churches do not have the financial and people resources to provide such a variety of services. Often feeling overwhelmed and helpless leads church leaders to not responding at all.

A lbertini
You are correct. In most cases such services are not delivered in traditional church settings, rather in rehabilitative and residential treatment settings. The question to ask is how might the church help in facilitating the provision of such services to help more people in need. Persons who are affected by such complex problems are in need of not just mental or emotional help but spiritual healing of their souls. Too often, the churches are left completely out of the equation when community-based interventions are designed and provided. For instance, the church buildings become a place where homeless people go to beg but not to find connections to resources that help to tear down strongholds in their lives.

G renz
Pastors and church leaders need to understand that to minister more comprehensively to the needs of people who are homeless or addicted; they need to partner with others in social service agencies in their communities. While pastoring in a community in Alberta, Canada, I saw this partnership work to make a difference. Out of our ministerial network, we appointed pastors and other church leaders to serve on the boards of almost all the social service agencies in our community. These board members mobilized the churches in the community to partner actively with the work of these agencies. In turn, many of these agencies helped to inform and equip individuals in churches to reach out to those affected by poverty and addictions. A key to this partnership was the change in understanding volunteerism. Often pastors and church leaders see volunteering in ministry as only activities within the church. For us, it also meant that we had to expand our understanding of volunteerism beyond the church walls.

A lbertini
It seems like you had some remarkable experiences in your church in Canada. I find myself thinking about the church's vision that Pastor Starr com-

mented about in the case study, the vision for a daycare center at the church. He saw the social problems in the community as a threat to the church's vision. He also said, "We knew we would have some of that problem when we bought the church-property at such a low price, in the heart of the inner-city. The issue isn't the people; it is deciding just how many of the social problems we are to take on. I also have trouble sleeping at nights just dealing with the feelings of not having done enough at the end of the day." It seems to me that he did not realize that a large number of school-age children exist among homeless families. Children make up a large segment of our nation's homeless population. Homeless people, including those who are addicted to drugs and alcohol, have children who are in need of good Christian education. Christian education might be part of the solution to breaking the cycle of poverty—homelessness, substance abuse and addictions in our communities. The church's vision for a school in their neighborhood was developed; it seems, without consideration for some of the most vulnerable children in the surrounding community, the homeless. One might argue that it is not the responsibility of church leaders to address such social problems in a church setting. Such might be the case, but church leaders and their congregation can certainly set the tone and influence the attitudes and behaviors of those in their community who are responsible for serving homeless families.

G renz
Some churches have changed their location because of the changing demographics of the community around the church. It is interesting that Pastor Starr didn't consider the characteristics of the community when they developed the vision. I believe that when developing a vision for a church, we need to consider that God's vision for our ministry often involves those living in the area where God has placed us. For Pastor Starr's church, this means developing a vision and a ministry strategy that might also serve those who are homeless and/or addicted. At the same time, I want to say that location does not release us of our responsibility to the homeless and addicted if our church is not in a community struggling with these issues.

Conclusion

This chapter's case study dealt with some very pressing issues in society—homelessness, and drug dependence and abuse. Using Pastors Broen and Starr's conversation as an example, we can explore the dilemma that some church leaders might face as they attempt to confront such problems in urban settings. Many of the same problems exist in rural areas, though experienced differently in that geographic context. With a deeper look into the matter of homelessness, drug and alcohol addictions and the need to develop partnerships by networking with social service providers, we see how social workers might assist church leaders in dealing with the problems and in fulfilling the missions of urban churches.

In the next chapter, there is an opportunity to explore yet another pressing social issue. In fact, that problem is so huge—it is a pandemic. You might have already guessed that it is the world-wide problem caused by HIV/AIDS. Chapter Three allows readers to learn more about the personal and social challenges facing people who are diagnosed with HIV and AIDS-related illnesses. The problems associated with AIDS are too complex and multifaceted for us to have covered completely in one book, much less in a single chapter. The aim here is not to cover the topic exhaustively but simply to continue to show the benefits of collaboration between pastors and social workers. In fact, the discussions stemming from the case study in the chapter will deal primarily with problems on a personal and social level. Each reader is encouraged to extrapolate salient information from the case study that he or she might find useful for understanding the problem on a broader scale.

CHAPTER 3

What If I Catch It?

Introduction

In this chapter, the case study draws our attention towards a most challenging area of Church ministries; that involves pastoral care with people facing illnesses and death related to Human Immunodeficiency Viruses or Acquired Immune Deficiency Syndrome (HIV/AIDS). We explore responses which churches and church leaders might take in showing grace and mercy to many who are suffering in secret and living in fear of being stigmatized or ostracized within Christian communities. Depicted in the case study is a conversation between a pastor and a parishioner who reports that he is dying of AIDS. A conversation of this kind could very well take place in almost any city or community in the world. Ever since the first HIV/AIDS cases were identified in the 1980s, the epidemic has been spreading to almost every part of our country. Today few people remain unaware of the devastation caused by the various strains of HIV viruses.

Recent figures in the U.S. reveal that there are over 40,000 new cases added annually. Most of the people who are infected with HIV viruses, range in age 25 years and younger. New infections, especially among women, are increasing daily. The AIDS epidemic is definitely no longer a crisis just for a few people or health professionals to be concerned about.[1] HIV/AIDS is confronting all people groups and organizations including the church. Most ministries across the world, if they have not already done so, will inevitably encounter the need to engage in some sort of social activism on the part of people affected by HIV/AIDS. Take, for instance, excerpts from a website posting placed on the Saddleback Church in Lake Forest, California, where Kay Warren is the co-founder and executive director of the church's HIV/AIDS Initiative. Using the website, Warren calls attention to the church's national and international mission of ministering to people affected by HIV/AIDS. Just imagine if all churches in the U.S. were to offer a similar welcome to the one posted on the Saddleback' website. It states:

> "Welcome to the HIV Caring Community *website!* If this is your first time to visit, be sure to look through the archived issues for helpful information about how your church can begin an HIV ministry [and learn] firsthand account of a woman who toured the World Vision Experience...You'll be touched by the story of a man with a secret who finally decided that he was through hiding...While HIV/AIDS is an incurable disease, there are at least six ways that every church can engage in the fight: Care for and comfort the sick - Handle testing and counseling - Unleash a force of volunteers - Remove the stigma - Champion healthy behavior - Help with nutrition and medications.[2]

As Christians we are all called to show God's love and mercy to all people including those infected and affected by HIV/AIDS (Mt 25:31-46).

Case Study: Luke's Battle with AIDS

"He died before he died"[3]

◘The Reverend Browne pastors a local church in the inner-city. One afternoon as he was leaving his office and heading home to his family, he witnessed something out of the ordinary in the church's parking lot. As he glanced across the lot, he spotted a middle-aged man slumped over the steering wheel of a parked car and he appeared to be sobbing. As the pastor drew closer, the figure in the car grew more familiar. In fact, he knew him; it was Luke. Luke is a new parishioner who began attending services at the church about six months prior to this encounter. Reverend Browne rapped on the window of the car and offered Luke the opportunity to go inside to talk about what it was that was troubling him so intensely. Upon returning to his office, Pastor Browne offered Luke a bottle of water as they began to talk. After a brief moment of silence, Luke gained his composure and began sharing his story. He spoke uninterrupted for the better part of half an hour. As Luke began to talk he said, "Pastor, I might as well tell it to you straight out. I am dying."

"What do you mean?" the pastor asked with a puzzled look on his face.

Luke went on to report how he had found out about eleven months earlier that he had the virus that causes AIDS. "I haven't told anyone. Not even my family knows."

"Have you shared this with your ex-wife?" asked Pastor Browne

No pastor, not even her. I've been trying for months but I can't seem to find a way to tell her. I tried so many times but the words never come out. I know how much she will suffer once she finds out. I also know that she will tell other people in the family, and I'm still not ready for that. I have been so afraid of facing it all alone, but not even my mother knows. My mother has a bad heart and if she finds out it will surely kill her. I know that I have to tell my ex-wife because she too is at risk [sob]. You see many years ago, I had an affair with another woman and that is how I got the virus.

"Even though I've asked God for forgiveness a million times, I'm not sure God hears me. I keep praying for a miracle but still I'm scared out of my mind. I'm taking all sorts of medications but the doctors aren't exactly sure I'll be able to make it. I apologize for taking up your time so late in the evening and for bringing all this heavy stuff down on you, but you caught me at a bad time. I usually come here to just sit in the car outside the church and pray but it's been a hard day. I haven't slept in days; I have no desire to eat, sleep or anything. Pastor, do you think God will forgive someone like me when I die? It's a hard thing to be dying of AIDS. I feel so desperate to have to keep this secret to myself. Some days I feel like my life is already over, so why not just end it. I come here just to sit and pray, some days just so as not to give in and kill myself. I thank you so much for listening. Today was one of my roughest days. I'm not sure I would have been able to talk myself out of ending it all tonight.

Theological Reflections: Checking our "gut" theologies

*"Behold, there came a leper and worshipped Him, saying,
Lord, if thou wilt, thou canst make me clean."
Matthew 8:2*

As readers review the case study, they should note that the voice and comments of the Reverend Browne were kept to a minimum. The aim is to allow the narrative to continue uninterrupted. From a biblical and theological perspective, your first thoughts as a Christian leader and minister might have centered on the importance of showing love, grace and mercy to Luke. Perhaps your first response was to empathize or to consider what it would be like if you were in a desperate situation and needed badly to share a heavy burden. In ministering to people or a person with HIV/AIDS, maybe instead of thinking of grace and mercy, we might find ourselves with thoughts of negative judgments, but it bodes well to remember that all of us at one time or another will be in need of God's grace and mercy. As the Apostle Paul reminds us in the Book of Hebrews: "Let us then approach the throne of grace with confidence, so that we may receive mercy and find grace to help us in our time of need."[4]

Some might be thinking that the person who has contracted HIV is just reaping the consequences of his or her sinful behavior. Some might be struck with fears of catching HIV/AIDS from someone who is infected, unsure of how to respond to the person's needs. Paul's teaching on grace and mercy calls us to deal with such thoughts and feelings by addressing our "gut" theology and connecting with Jesus' ministry of mercy. Each one of us has a set of "gut" theologies to guide us, but we are largely unaware of them. Our "gut" theologies come out in our thoughts, words and actions. When it comes to HIV, we believe we need first to become aware of our "gut" theologies related to sickness in general and then to HIV/AIDS. Here are some of the thoughts or sayings that might express one's "gut" theologies about sickness:

"This is God's punishment for sin."
"This is just the devil attacking you."
"This is the Lord's will, and His will be done."
"This is a test."
"This is just a part of life's woes."

Let us take, for instance, the narrative concerning the man called Job from the Book of Job in the Old Testament; we find Job's friends who came to console their afflicted friend demonstrate similar "gut" theologies.[5] For example, Bildad says to Job:

"How long will you say such things? Your words are a blustering wind. Does God pervert justice? Does the Almighty pervert what is right? When your children sinned against him, he gave them over to the penalty of their sin. But if you will look to God and plead with the Almighty, if you are pure and upright, even now he will rouse himself on your behalf and restore you to your rightful place." (Jb 8:2-6)

Sickness and death, according to Bildad, were a penalty for sin and if Job just confessed his sin and became pure, God would raise him. This perspective also appears in the New Testament when the disciples question Jesus about the man blind from birth. They asked Jesus, *"Rabbi, who sinned, this man or his parents, that he was born blind?"* (Jn 9:2). These "gut" theologies lead us to address the causes of sickness from a theological perspective. Hoffman and Grenz highlight three main causes of sickness.[6]

The first cause of sickness is the result of our contact with a fallen environment. The Apostle Paul writes that creation is in a fallen state and not in the perfect order that God intended for it.[7] This means that this fallen environment brings illness and death to us. Anglican Bishop J. C. Ryle puts it this way: "Sickness is everywhere. . . . A man's house is called his castle; but there are no doors and barricades which can keep out disease and death."[8] The second cause is related to the sins of society. As members of a specific group or nation, we are disposed to sicknesses that arise out of lifestyle characteristics of our society. For example, the frenzied pace of our Western society has been connected to illnesses like high blood pressure, heart disease, and even certain varieties of cancer. The last cause of sickness is related to personal sin. This refers to sickness that is a result of a person's involvement in risky activities or behavior. For example, a person who smokes is prone to lung cancer or a person who is an alcoholic is prone to liver problems.

Hoffman and Grenz also state, "In the Bible, specific sicknesses were sometimes allowed by God as an indication of God's displeasure concerning sin present in a person's life and as a warning that repentance is needed."[9] These causes of sickness relate to the HIV/AIDS epidemic. For the most part, it is an easy conclusion that HIV infections are related to personal sin. "Homosexual activities, heterosexual promiscuity, and I.V. drug abuse do place an individual into a high-risk category, as medical research has demonstrated."[10] There is a strong connection between actions and consequences. However, we must be careful not to jump too quickly to judge. It seems that too often we are quick to judge HIV infection while not addressing the same cause and effect relationship between smoking and lung cancer. HIV/AIDS is not only related to personal sin, it relates to societal sin. How much is the spread of HIV a result of values of our society? It would be fair to say that our American society is dominated by sex and self-gratification. "Given these twin emphases—the glorification of sexual pleasure and the quest for greater thrills in general—it is not surprising that HIV/AIDS would quickly reach epidemic proportions in America."[11] Our prophetic voice needs to address our society as well as individuals.

There are two other issues related to our "gut" theologies that we need to address. First, we need to ask ourselves, What about those who contract HIV apart from any involvement in risky lifestyle? For example, there are hemophiliacs who have been infected through blood-product transfusions or babies who have been born with this infection and heterosexual couples who are infected. Hoffman and Grenz write, "For the Christian, this means that HIV/AIDS cannot be viewed merely as a moral issue. . . . It is a disease, an enemy of humanity, and therefore is to be fought like all other enemies. Nor (as we have seen) can we view AIDS as solely a 'gay problem.' Rather, it is a human problem."[12] The second issue is related to us as the community of God's people, and particularly to us as Christian leaders. What might God be saying to us during this epidemic? Often our focus is outward when we consider HIV, but we need to examine ourselves. "To what degree are homosexually oriented persons driven to the gay community because they are unable to find help within the wider society and more specifically within our churches? To what extent have Christians been guilty of sinning against persons with a homosexual orientation because of our failure to show love and to offer them the true fellowship they are seeking?"[13] As a community of God, we are compelled to examine our role in this epidemic as well as our role in responding too slowly to the epidemic. This leads us to explore a theological basis for our response in ministry.

Connecting with mercy

Our "gut" theologies form many of the barriers that hinder ministry to those inflicted with HIV. As Christian leaders and as a community of God's people, we are called to overcome these barriers. We can overcome these barriers by connecting to HIV infected individuals with mercy. Mercy is a deeply felt love or compassion for a fellow human being, especially for those who are suffering. The New Testament challenges us with Jesus' merciful acts and his teachings on mercy. Throughout the Gospels, Jesus encounters individuals who are in great need. When thinking about HIV/AIDS, many look to Jesus' response to those with leprosy. One such encounter is recorded in three of the Gospels.[14] A man inflicted with leprosy approaches Jesus and pleads with Jesus to heal him. Jesus responded to the request by reaching down and touching him, saying, "I am willing. Be clean!" Healing is a merciful act, but so is touching the man with leprosy. It is amazing to know that Jesus crossed laws forbidding any physical contact with lepers. It's even more amazing knowing that Jesus didn't even need to touch the man to heal him. Jesus chose to reach out and touch people with leprosy when everyone else was afraid to go near them.

Not only does Jesus demonstrate mercy; he also challenges his followers to be merciful to others. When teaching about loving your enemies, Jesus says, "Be merciful, just as your Father is merciful." (Lk 6:36). We are to put forth mercy and act mercifully to others, especially those who are suffering. This is the challenge of ministry to those with HIV/AIDS.

In an article on caring for those with HIV/AIDS, Neville Richardson writes, A key ecclesiological question to be asked in the face of HIV/AIDS could be expressed as an adaptation of Martin Luther's famous question that sparked Reformation faith and doctrine. In his early spiritual struggles, Luther agonized: "Where can I find a merciful God?" In our context, the question might be rephrased as: "Where can we find a caring church?" For it would seem contradictory to claim to be a group of people joined by a common allegiance to Jesus Christ and not to be actively caring, embodying compassion, for those at hand with HIV/AIDS, who are in desperate need.[15]

For early Christians, mercy was a foundation for ministry. Paul includes mercy as a spiritual gift. This does not mean that merciful acts are only for those who are gifted with mercy, but it means that some have been specially endowed with extraordinary ability to express mercy. Paul also commands the Christians in Colossae to be merciful. *"Since God chose you to be the holy people he loves, you must clothe yourselves with tenderhearted mercy, kindness, humility, gentleness, and patience."* (Col 3:12, NLT). James states that heavenly wisdom is characterized by mercy.[16] Therefore, when wondering how to respond to someone in need, true wisdom would be full of mercy.

In summary, checking our "gut" theologies calls us to avoid judging those with HIV, but to realize that this disease creates a group of individuals who are in great need of ministry. Judgment should be replaced with grace. Grace should be accompanied with mercy, for we see that Jesus modeled and taught a ministry of mercy. Therefore, above all else, put on grace and mercy.

Connecting Pastoral Care and Social Work

With the Luke case study, we are able to consider some key concerns for individuals and families who are infected or affected by HIV/AIDS and explore the role of the church. As with the previous case study in Chapter One, our focus rests on finding a proper balance between meeting the social and psychological needs of people in need without losing sight of our primary role of delivering the gospel. Luke presented issues of suffering, shame, doubt, grief, death and God's forgiveness. Although very few details were provided concerning the pastor's role, it is important that we do recognize the opportunity he had to explore resources that might be available in the church as well as in the community to address Luke's crisis and his ongoing needs. Armed with Christ's message of hope, Pastor Browne would no doubt be able to counsel and pray with Luke at that very moment. However, given some of the thoughts and feelings that Luke expressed, it is very important to make referral to professionals trained in clinical counseling.

For instance, Pastor Browne would need to know whether Luke has access to social workers, or other mental health counselors. Many today are unaware of how naturally church outreach ministries and social work practices fit together, especially when it comes to serving people with HIV/AIDS. "Core professional values embraced by social workers include provision of services for all in need, advocating for and seeking social justice for all, upholding the dignity and worth of all people, recognizing the importance of human relationships, serving with integrity, and competence."[17] Those core values make collaborations between pastoral care and social work more compatible.

Luke's case study allows us to focus on experiences that are similar to those of Jesus' time, when He ministered to ostracized people. When we encounter individuals or families infected or affected by HIV/AIDS, it is important not only to recognize the spiritual, psychological, physical and social dimensions of the problems but also help to curtail stigmas associated with the disease. The case study offers an opportunity to explore the following questions.

Reality Dialogue Questions

Should church leaders be proactive in seeking out men, women and children living with HIV/AIDS, in order to minister to them; or is it best to let them seek us out; or is it just best to leave such matters to others agencies? Should churches collaborate with other community organizations that serve people with HIV/AIDS?

Those of us who serve in pastoral care and outreach ministries will inevitably have numerous opportunities to minister to the spiritual and social needs of people who are sick, including those living with HIV/AIDS. However, simply having the opportunities does not necessarily guarantee that we will recognize or even accept such opportunities. The sheer growth of the HIV/AIDS epidemic suggests that there are ample opportunities for ministry with people who are affected. [18] Indeed, as pastors and church outreach ministers, we have much to offer the sick, particularly given the examples we have to draw upon through the life of Christ. In New Testament Scriptures, we find Jesus often going out of His way to find and minister to sick and ostracized people of his society. For instance, he reached out to people society labeled as lepers, the demon-possessed, fornicators and adulterers. [19]

Churches exist in communities where many people with HIV/AIDS are living and dying; therefore, we cannot ignore the problem. We need to acknowledge that HIV/AIDS is not just something happening outside the walls of our churches. People in churches today are living with HIV/AIDS or have family members or friends living with related diseases. Those infected need us to open our eyes to the problem, break our tradition of silence and acknowledge the painful reality. Rather than living in fear or holding a moralistic approach to the diseases, there is a great need for us to reach out actively to those inside and outside the walls of the church. Relinquishing our fears of AIDS might be easier said than done, it also involves us breaking out of our comfort-zones to be the hands, feet, and voice of the grace and healing power of Jesus Christ.

Yes, every single church, regardless of size, should develop ministry relationships with workers and volunteers in community organizations that are on the frontline fighting against the deadly diseases that have devastated so many lives. Many churches are behind the times in terms of knowledge and information about HIV/AIDS.

Synergistic Dialogue:

"Are not five sparrows sold for two pennies?
Yet not one of them is forgotten"
Luke 12:6

G renz
Despite good research and education, there still seem to be a great deal of stigmas and fears attached to HIV/AIDS, even among Christians. HIV/AIDS carries a stigma that other diseases do not and it goes beyond the transmission of the HIV viruses. Some Christians fail to reach out to those in need because they are fearful that their actions might communicate that they are condoning sinful actions. Some might fear that those infected with AIDS might be prone to failure and fall back into destructive behaviors. We need to move beyond our fears and step out to make a difference. Luke 12:6 reminds us that no one is insignificant in the sight of God; thus individuals and families in need should be high on our list of top priorities.

A lbertini
I agree that much work remains to remove stigmas associated with HIV/AIDS. I can still remember the very first time I counseled someone whom I knew had tested positive for HIV. I met with the person in the early 1990s, before I completed my graduate training in social work. I can still remember my trepidations about the first counseling session. Back then people did not know as much as we do now about how HIV is contracted. Despite the fact that I was working in a secular setting, I knew that I had to rely on the teachings of Christ to overcome my fears and in order to show my client all the grace, love and professionalism that all clients deserve. As I reflect back, I am glad that my "gut" theology on sickness included the showing of grace and compassion, regardless of the nature of the sickness. As years passed, the medical community and researchers found that there is nothing to fear in counseling relationships with persons living with HIV and AIDS. In fact, it is the persons with HIV immune systems that are compromised—not those of non-infected people. If anything, they are more at risk from their exposure to us. Something as simple as the common cold, which they could easily contract from us, could prove devastating for their weakened immune systems. People encountered some of the same fear we face today in Jesus' time; he indeed touched and healed the lepers of his time when no one else would do so.

G renz
When we embody the Fruit of the Spirit, we are better able to extend grace and friendship to those living with HIV/AIDS. However, what does this look like? It simply looks like reaching out and treating each person like everyone

else. It is treating them with respect and not heaping more shame on them. It is listening to their frustration and grief. When necessary, it is teaching them about God's forgiveness. All this is instrumental to helping individuals experience community and freedom of guilt and shame. From an institutional standpoint, the challenge for churches is developing the ability to be advocates for those suffering with HIV/AIDS. This is difficult for many, because a number of the local and national advocacy groups might have strong beliefs that are contrary to our Christian beliefs. I believe that some Christians are not in a position to be advocates for HIV/AIDS infected individuals due to deep-seated fears.

Albertini

Not all churches will be the same in terms of the way they organize their network of resources. We are certainly not suggesting that all churches should launch an HIV/AIDS response program, such as the one at the Saddleback church. We are however, encouraging more churches to play active roles in caring for those in their communities who are dying with AIDS and influencing how their communities respond. Many health and social service programs exist in communities to address social problems related to HIV/AIDS; we are calling Christian leaders to be present at the decision table to influence how people affected by HIV/AIDS are to be treated in their communities. The AIDS pandemic has created unique opportunities for us to show Jesus' unconditional love to the world. If we are to "think globally and act locally" to halt the devastating effects of AIDS, then our ministry starts just beyond our church walls. I owe a debt of gratitude to the very first person diagnosed with the HIV virus, whom I had the privilege of counseling. It was while working as a social work intern, in the community, that I discovered my "gut" theology for ministry with such courageous people. People with HIV cope with society's stigma while at the same time dealing with all of the physical and psychological issues related to sickness and death. I will never forget the counselee who informed me about a church in Fort Lauderdale that ministers to people during and after their incarceration in prisons. After visiting the church several times, I became an active member and served alongside the pastoral team as a church social worker for fifteen years. I can remember at the onset of that ministry experience, expressing to the senior pastor that I had received my training as a social worker at a secular university but felt God's calling to do church social work. The senior pastor not only welcomed me; he inspired me to integrate Christ's teachings into my social work training as I served in the church. I am forever grateful to that pastor for his confidence in my skills and calling. While serving at the church I continued my education and eventually became a university professor of social work. I later partnered with another professor and conducted a major community-based ethnographic study of culturally relevant strategies for serving persons in the community who are living with HIV/AIDS. The results of that study provided culturally relevant strategies for workers and ministers in secular and faith-based organizations who are addressing the needs of people with HIV/AIDS. I shared this story to illustrate how one might engage both the church and community in responding locally to such a global social problem.

Conclusion

There will always be opportunities for collaboration among those who serve within Christian communities, especially when it comes to fighting the devastating effects of HIV/AIDS on individuals, families and communities. In fact, today's church leaders cannot afford to ignore the problems associated with HIV/AIDS or hold to the belief that church-goers are immune from such effects, directly or indirectly. From a preparedness standpoint, all pastors need to develop biblically-based plans of action to help individuals and families who are touched by HIV-related diseases. Church leaders who understand how to address the spiritual questions related to AIDS with a sound biblical foundation are invaluable to their churches and communities. Even more valuable are pastors who are able to address the spiritual, and at the same time connect people who are affected, to community resources that meet their physical and emotional needs. From a social action standpoint, it is important that we all join forces with those in Christian communities who are already reaching out to those affected by the diseases. Here again partnerships with local social workers would enhance the effectiveness of helping relationships that develop in church settings. Social workers naturally understand how to develop and utilize community resources, and pastors naturally understand the spiritual dimensions of caring for those affected by diseases. In addition, social workers are excellent resources because they are able to assist by assessing the needs of individuals and families, and to help them to connect with necessary social services. It is for those reasons that we call for more collaboration between pastors and social workers in the battle against HIV/AIDS. In Chapter Four, questions are raised about another social problem that presents challenges for church leaders and society. The problem is domestic violence, also referred to as intimate partner violence.

CHAPTER 4

I Wasn't Trained for This!

Introduction

In the time it takes you to read this sentence, another woman will have experienced physical abuse at the hand of her husband or boyfriend. Approximately every twelve seconds, a woman in the U.S. is battered.[1] Domestic violence, also known as intimate partner violence, is the leading cause of injuries for women between the ages of fifteen and forty-four years; we know all this from reports of the U.S. Surgeon General's Office. Injuries related to domestic violence occur more commonly than automobile accidents, and muggings.[2] The American Psychological Association Presidential Force on Violence and Family predicts that about one in every three women will experience some form of domestic violence during her lifetime. Husbands and intimate partners will perpetrate fifty percent of the violence, and more than a third will occur in multiple episodes.[3] Domestic violence continues to present unique challenges for those working to address the needs of victims as well as perpetrators. Neither churches nor social service organizations can afford to ignore domestic violence and its devastating effects on families in our society.

What exactly is Domestic Violence?

During a major campaign launched against domestic violence in 1987, it became necessary to designate October as Domestic Violence Awareness Month. The problem was serious enough that in 1989 the U.S. Congress moved to enact a law supporting the choice of the month for Domestic Violence Awareness nation-wide. As the campaign progressed, in October 1994, the National Coalition Against Domestic Violence, an activist organization that collects information on the victims who are killed annually by intimate partners, began producing annual listings of names and pictures of those who are killed each year. By 1996, a much-awaited national toll-free hotline (1-800-799-SAFE) was launched to receive calls from and about victims.[4] Despite all efforts to inform the public about domestic violence, including the creation of the national hotline and availability of numerous websites focusing on the violence, some in the public remains unaware of the nature of domestic violence.

> It involves a pattern of abusive behavior towards another person or persons. Such behavior involve physical, sexual, and psychological attacks as well as economic coercion—used by one intimate partner against another (adult or adolescent) to gain, maintain, or regain power and control in the relationship. Batterers use a range of tactics to frighten, terrorize, manipulate, hurt, humiliate, blame, often injure, and sometimes kill a current or former intimate partner.[5]

Today there are more resources and materials available to workers in churches and other organizations to equip those willing to help victims of domestic abuse. Still, there is much more work to be done to prepare church leaders and workers to combat the devastating effect of domestic violence for those who turn to churches for help. Albert Einstein, in commenting on the condition of the world, once said, "The world is a dangerous place to live; not because of the people who are evil, but because of the people who don't do anything about it." Our aim in this chapter is to inform the Christian community about domestic violence and suggest ways to respond.

The people's story and circumstances depicted in the upcoming case study sheds light on some of the challenges ministers might face while helping victims of domestic violence. We emphasize two caveats for our readers; the first is that they realize that even though the story presents a woman as the victim, men are also victims of such abuse. Second, the story portrays a law enforcement officer as the abuser; however, the case study could have easily depicted an abuser from another profession. Domestic violence affects people from all professional, ethnic, cultural, religious, and geographic backgrounds.[6] The case study raises awareness about the nature of the problem and prompts readers to look toward a collaborative approach that involves pastors, social workers and other trained responders.

Case study: What if he kills her?

■It was a brisk Easter Sunday morning and Pastor Brinkley was preaching one of the most compelling sermons that Janet had ever heard concerning the empowering grace of God that equips the church for her mission. Up until that morning, Janet had never thought deeply about the church's role in reaching out to suffering families. She already understood the church's role in spreading the gospel but not in ministering so directly to people where they live. The sermon meant more to Janet than anyone might realize. People who knew her often spoke about how gifted she was as a school teacher or complimented her for having a calm demeanor when dealing with children. Seeing Janet, no one in her circle of friends would ever have guessed the heavy burdens she bore. Janet had begun attending youth group meetings at Pastor Brinkley's church as a teenager. She was the only one in her family to attend church on a regular basis. In fact, it was at an annual church picnic that Janet, then twenty-three years old, met and later married her husband Tom. Tom was twenty-eight years old and he had been working as a law enforcement officer for about three years. Despite his age, Tom had already been married twice before he met Janet. Both of his prior marriages had ended in bitter divorces. Tom and Janet were hoping for success in their marriage. At first, Tom was a model spouse; he was loving and attentive, and so was Janet. Then, shortly after celebrating their second wedding anniversary, Janet began noticing that their relationship was being affected by changes in Tom's mood. In addition, Tom was working very long hours, experiencing a great deal of work-related stress, and he resumed an old habit of drinking excessive amounts of alcohol on his days off. Tom often said that drinking calmed his nerves after a hectic week at the police station. Janet's worries increased when she discovered from friends that Tom's other marriages had deteriorated after his drinking got out of control.

During their third year of marriage, Tom and Janet found themselves arguing frequently over what they themselves called petty issues. Often the arguments involved one telling the other about dissatisfactions about the other's behaviors or their relationship. One Friday evening during just such an argument, Janet decided to express concerns about Tom's drinking. In response to her comments, Tom told Janet to stuff it, a phrase he often used when he wanted a discussion to end. He also told Janet that it was none of her business what he did in his own house on his days off. He also criticized her for being an ungrateful woman. He argued that he worked and put up with stuff on his job just to put a roof over her head and that she had no right to complain. In a desperate attempt to convince Tom of the validity of her feelings, Janet told him that she did not want to be married to a drunk. Tom responded with some unsavory words, to which Janet said that their marriage was a big mistake.

The comment infuriated Tom to the point where he could hardly find words to respond. He simply looked at Janet, slammed his palm down on the table where he was sitting and got up to leave the room. To Janet it appeared as if he was heading for the garage; it wasn't unusual for him to storm out or to jump in his car and drive away. As he passed the kitchen counter, Tom grabbed up his car keys. Thinking about how much he had been drinking, Janet reached out her hand and asked Tom not to drive in his condition. Without giving her a chance to finish her sentence, Tom angrily shoved her out of his way, up against a hallway wall and left. Up until that moment, he had never had a physical altercation with Janet. Yes, he has been angry but never violent. The incident left Janet startled. Emotionally shaken by the incident, she realized that she had experienced a side to her husband she had never seen before.

Tom would later say that Janet's comments about their marriage set him off and that he interpreted her actions as an insult to his manhood. Later that same month during another heated argument, Tom's anger led to his slapping Janet across her head, causing her to knock her face against a bookshelf. The blow broke her nose and bruised her cheekbone. Even after seeing her fall, Tom proceeded to shout profanities at Janet, and demanded that she stay out of his business. Seeing her swollen face, he later pointed out that Janet had caused the injuries. He said, "See what your mouth brought on." When his anger subsided and he saw the seriousness of the injury to Janet's face, Tom tried to console his wife with apologizes and promises that he would never raise his hand against her again. In his attempt to show remorse, he offered to get her an icepack, and even decided that he would order a pizza for dinner.

By the following day, Janet was still experiencing excruciating pain; her face was black and blue. Fearing that her nose was more than likely broken, Janet reluctantly asked Tom if he would drive her to the nearby hospital's emergency room. Seeing her face, he agreed to take Janet to the hospital but cautioned her to be careful in answering questions of the medical staff. He commented that as a police officer he had seen many good people's lives ruined over misunderstanding like what had occurred. Janet agreed to go along with Tom's suggestion that she tell everyone that she tripped and fell while climbing up and reaching for a box in her garage. Tom made sure that Janet synchronized details of their story with the nature of her injuries. Despite her struggle to control feelings of shame, anger, and insecurity, Janet acted her part and Tom presented himself as a concerned and attentive husband. When they returned home, Tom declared that Janet's action at the hospital protected not only his career but their family and for that, he was grateful. Tom again asked for forgiveness, and swore he would never lay a hand on Janet again. Sadly, Tom did not keep his promise for very long.

Within a matter of weeks, he resumed heavy drinking and abusing Janet physically and emotionally. With each incident, Janet grew more fearful for her life but told no one of the abuse. A few times Tom would threaten to blow Janet's head off if she tried to leave him. With each event, she considered calling the police for help but relented since most of the officers in her area were friends of Tom or knew of him. Janet rationalized her abuse. She blamed the stress of his job for his mood changes and decided against jeopardizing his career by reporting the incidents. One Friday, while Tom was still at work, Janet decided to pay a visit to Pastor Brinkley at the church. She remembered the message he preached about the empowering work of God's spirit. Janet hoped that her pastor would be able to give her some advice concerning Tom.

Janet's story of abuse caught her pastor off guard. None of the details seemed to fit with the image he had of her and her husband. Never would he have guessed that Janet was living in such fear for her life. After praying with Janet, Pastor Brinkley asked several questions about her experience. He also inquired whether anyone in her family was aware of the abuse. He asked whether she believed her husband would be open to the idea of counseling. Startled by his last question, Janet insisted that she did not want her husband to find out that she came for guidance. Janet's intention was to return home to try to handle the matter herself. She also shared that her purpose for telling the pastor was to ensure that someone else knew just in case something terrible happened in her home. She felt better just knowing that someone else knew her secret. Hearing Janet's intentions, the pastor agreed to keep their conversation in confidence. Janet's report of violence was so compelling that he encouraged her in no uncertain terms to call 9-1-1 right away should she sense that her life was at risk. He also admonished her not to give up in efforts to win back her husband's heart, using her gentle spirit. After Janet left, the pastor prayed for her safety but remained puzzled about ways to help her and her husband.

Theological Reflections: Loving, Cherishing, and Leaving no Place for Abuse

"Rescue me, O Lord, from evil men; protect me from men of violence" Psalms 140:2:7

Of the many social problems church leaders face, domestic violence is one of the most misunderstood, when it come to helping victims. Many pastors have no training in dealing with this issue, and as a result, make the situation worse, not better. Evangelical leaders wrestle with questions that make it difficult to minister to victims of domestic violence and address oppressors—questions like, Should wives submit to their husbands, even if they are abusers?—Is separation or divorce a biblical response to domestic violence? A great way to begin a theological reflection on this section is by exploring how the Bible views abusers or oppressors.

There are several times when the Bible condemns powerful men for abusing the weak and vulnerable. The psalmist states, "The LORD examines the righteous, but the wicked and those who love violence his soul hates. On the wicked he will rain fiery coals and burning sulfur; a scorching wind will be their lot" (Ps 11:5-6). Isaiah 1:15-17 clearly states that God does not listen to the prayers of those who have been violent and oppressive; instead, He calls the people to encourage the oppressed and defend the fatherless and widows. Of the various characteristics of people addressed during the "last days," Paul includes those who are abusive (2 Tm 3:1-7). He instructs Timothy to have nothing to do with such people. Oppression and violence are things that God detests and warns against (Prv 6:16-17; Jer 22:7; Ez 18:10-13; 22:7, 27-20; Rom 3:14-17). All of those Scriptures indicate God's stance against all forms of abuse.

Paul also provides a command more specifically to husbands in Colossians 3:19: "Husbands, love your wives and do not be harsh with them." This verse, along with Paul's instructions to husbands in Ephesians 5:25-32 (instructing husbands to care for and respect their wives just as Christ did the church), leaves no room for excusing a husband's violent and abusive behavior toward his wife. "Christian husbands are not to become angry or incensed against their wives, either in thought or in word and deed."[8] Rather, husbands are commanded to nurture their wives and care for them (Eph 5:25, 28-29, 33; Col 3:19). There are corresponding scriptures that instruct wives concerning their attitudes and behaviors toward their husbands, which also speak against abuses.

A number of theologians throughout the centuries state that suffering is a part of being a follower of Jesus, pointing to Jesus' suffering on the cross. 1 Peter 2:21-23 is often used as a primary support for this perspective. Elizabeth Rice Handford holds this position of female submission, stating that wives are to obey their husbands in everything, without qualification, even if a woman believes her husband's command goes against the will of God.[9] Thus, a Christian woman experiencing suffering through domestic violence should endure it as part of her accepting the suffering of the cross.

However, this view of suffering as it relates to domestic violence is missing in1 Peter 2. Christ's suffering on the cross is very different from the suffering one endures during domestic violence. Nancy Nienhuis outlines the differences. "First, Christ's going to the cross was a voluntary act. Second, the point of the cross was not the suffering but the resurrection. The idea was to display the power that transforms suffering, not to remain in it. If we are truly imitators of Christ, we will also work to transform the suffering around us. We will turn a theology of suffering into a theology of empowerment and life."[10] In addition, Peter is not teaching that all abuse is redemptive. Steven R. Tracy states that the "only kind of abuse that Peter recognizes as redemptive (having transforming spiritual value) is that which (1) is unavoidable and (2) is based on the victim's godly character."[11] Therefore, it is dangerous for pastors to use a theology of suffering to encourage victims to endure abusive relationships.

The subject of submission also can create difficulty when addressing domestic violence; especially as it is relates to wives submitting to their husbands. Colossians 3:18, Ephesians 5:22-24 and 1 Peter 3:1-6 are the biblical texts usually used when understanding submission of wives. Each text simply states that a wife is to submit to her husband just as she is to submit to Jesus Christ (Eph 5:22). The question pertinent to domestic violence that often challenges church leaders is; Does submission in marriage include submission to domestic violence or abuse? As mentioned previously, Elizabeth Rice Handford believes submission is submission in everything, even if it goes against the commands of God. Mary Kassian does not go as far as that in her argument. She writes, "Practically, there might be situations in which submission to authority is limited. However, these situations are few and far between. Our focus should be on humility and obedience to authority in all circumstances. Submission might indeed have limits, but these limits are the exception rather than the rule."[12]

Would domestic violence fall under these exceptions? To address this question, it is important to discuss one doctrinal issue and examine Ephesians 5:24. The doctrine of the lordship of Christ limits the authority of the husband. Christ's authority supersedes an earthly authority, including authority within family. Paul proclaims Jesus' supremacy over all things in Colossians 1:15-23. It is clear in this text that nothing or no one can supersede His authority. Jesus instructs his followers, "If anyone comes to me and does not hate his father and mother, his wife and children, his brothers and sisters—yes, even his own life— he cannot be my disciple" (Luke 14:26). Here he is making a strong statement about his lordship, which supersedes all family relationships and loyalties. Therefore, the extent of a husband's authority is limited, and both he and his wife are to surrender the lordship of Christ.

Paul gives the following instructions to wives: "Now as the church submits to Christ, so also wives should submit to their husbands in everything" (Eph 5:24). The key to this text is to understand how Paul describes the Church's submission to Christ; especially in the book of Ephesians. The Church looks to Christ as her head "for his beneficial rule [1:22], living by his norms, experiencing his presence [3:17] and love [3:19], receiving from him gifts [4:11-12] that will enable progress towards maturity [4:15-16], and responding to him in gratitude [5:19] and awe [5:21]."[13] Andrew T. Lincoln concludes, "In Ephesians the Church's submission to Christ is for the Church's benefit, enabling its growth, unity, and maturity, so that the wife's subordination to her husband also presupposes that it is part of a relationship in which the husband has her welfare constantly in view."[14] Based on this understanding, it seems this qualifier to the wife's submission to her husband would give a woman the option to escape from the abuse.

Another issue that arises when ministering to a woman or man encountering domestic violence is the issue of marital separation or divorce. For most evangelical leaders, marriage is held in high regard and separation and divorce are considered unacceptable. However, the issue of domestic violence causes many to reexamine their biblical understanding of separation and divorce.[15] This does not mean that one needs to ignore or twist the biblical texts to find a way to allow divorce for those who experience abuse. Prior to Jesus, the Old Testament allowed divorce for the breaking of marriage vows, including neglect and abuse, based on Exodus 21:10-11. While Exodus 21:10-11 deals specifically with a slave wife, Jewish law extended to free wives, based on the logic that if a slave wife had this right, a free wife would of course have the equivalent right.[16] David Instone-Brewer writes that the three rights outlined in this text, namely the right to food, clothing, and marital love, were later classified in rabbinic sources under two headings: material neglect and emotional neglect.[17] "Emotional neglect probably included much more than just lack of conjugal rights. Cruelty and humiliation were also recognized as grounds for divorce, and are related to emotional neglect in the Mishnah."[18]

However, some would suggest that Jesus dismisses the Old Testament view of divorce. Matthew 19:3-12 is a key biblical text used to support this claim. The

Pharisees tested Jesus, asking, "Is it lawful for a man to divorce his wife for any and every reason?"(v.3). During the Old Testament era there were two schools of thought on Moses' law in Deuteronomy 24:1.[19] The followers of Rabbi Hillel later interpreted this text to mean that a man could divorce his wife for any cause, while the followers of Rabbi Shammai held that marriage could be broken only by adultery.[20] The former interpretation of Deuteronomy 24:1 became known as "any cause" divorces. "The phrase 'for any cause' was a catchword in a raging debate in Jesus' day."[21] Instone-Brewer suggests that when the Pharisees asked Jesus this question they were asking if Jesus agreed with "any cause" divorces.[22] Therefore, he was not rejecting Moses' law, but rejecting the idea that a man could divorce his wife for any reason he wanted. Based on this discussion of divorce, we would conclude that domestic violence is grounds for the consideration of some kind of separation or divorce.

In conclusion, pastors and church leaders uphold the biblical view that oppression and abuse is detestable in the eyes of God; even within a marriage. We must understand that suffering produced by domestic violence is not to be equated with the suffering Jesus experienced on the cross. Finally, we should extend God's grace by giving allowance for separation or even divorce in cases of domestic violence that clearly threatens the life of a spouse.

Reality Dialogue Questions

What else might Pastor Brinkley and the church do to offer Janet help? Should Pastor Brinkley confront the abuser in Janet's case?

Pastor Brinkley must have done something correctly since Janet perceived him as someone she could go to for help. She was apparently comfortable enough to confide in him. He did what any good pastor would do; he listened and asked pertinent questions about her circumstances. Yet, the question remains, What might he do to ensure that Janet's worst fear does not come true? To understand the pastor's role in providing help, to victims of domestic violence, one needs to be aware of the nature of such abuse. As most pastors will attest, pastoral training does not always include preparation for dealing with domestic violence. While some churches might be equipped with trained personnel to address the needs of victims and abusers, most might have to rely on community resources. To rely on such resources pastors need to be aware of the places and people trained to help both parties, even if the help involves jail time for abusers.

The Synergistic Dialogue that follows provides more detail about responses to domestic violence. The aim here is to help readers to envision ways Pastor

Brinkley might guide Janet to a place of safety from the violence. Pastor Brinkley did well in conveying his concern about her safety and encouraging her to utilize the 9-1-1 services. It would have also been helpful if he had provided her with some resources specific to victim of domestic violence, such as the hotline number or addresses of nearby shelters for victims. Janet's actions suggest that she is expecting the violence to worsen; the pastor could have explored that matter further with Janet. The church might be an excellent resource for her as well. Churches have always been places of refuge for people in need. Often the self-esteem of the victim is low and she or he might experience feelings of disempowerment; it is, therefore, helpful to say to victims, "You deserve to be safe." Janet did not say whether she has a plan of escape should she find that her life is in eminent danger. Leaving Pastor Brinkley's office without a plan of escape might suggest that she remains vulnerable to her attacker. Neither Janet nor her pastor might be aware that the U.S. Department of Agriculture, Safety, Health, and Employee Welfare Division provides instructions for creating a Safety Plan. The plan presented below was adopted from a 1992 Preventing Domestic Violence Domestic Violence Awareness Handbook published by Laura Crites:

Creating a safety plan
1) Think about all possible escape routes (doors, first-floor windows, basement exits, elevators, stairwells); 2) Choose a place to go (home of a friend or relative who will offer unconditional support, or a motel or hotel, or a shelter - most importantly somewhere you will feel safe); 3) Pack a survival kit (money for cab fare, a change of clothes, extra house and car keys, birth certificates, passports, medications and copies of prescriptions, insurance information, checkbook, credit cards, legal documents such as separation agreements and protection orders, address books, and valuable jewelry, and papers that show jointly-owned assets. Conceal it all in the home or leave it with a trusted neighbor, friend, or relative. Important papers might also be left in a bank deposit box); 4 (Try to start an individual savings account. Have statements sent to a trusted relative or friend; 5) Avoid arguments with the abuser in areas with potential weapons (kitchen, garage, or in small spaces without access to an outside door); 6) Know the telephone number of the domestic violence hotline (Contact it for information on resources and legal rights); 7) Review the safety plan monthly.[23]

In regard to the question of whether to confront Janet's husband based on the information derived from the case study, Pastor Brinkley possesses no authority to confront Janet's abuser. Janet described her husband as someone who becomes violent when confronted. In addition, he is a trained and armed police officer who might not always abide by the law. There is need for further investigation concerning the violence; the question is who possesses the proper training to conduct such an investigation. It is very important that neither Janet nor anyone else is placed in further danger. Once trained professionals who can investigate the situation are involved, the decision *whether to, by whom* and *when to confront* will be addressed. In the meantime, Janet's safety and wellbeing is a top priority.

Synergistic Dialogue: Collaborative Responses

Many people are unaware that social workers operate in accordance with professional values that are deeply rooted in Judeo-Christian concepts of righteousness, justice and grace. A collaborative approach to domestic violence allows for an intersection of the roles and values of pastors with those of social workers. Each role complements the other. While pastoral care training might not include domestic violence awareness, the educational process for social workers amply prepares them to work with individuals and families affected by domestic violence. While social workers' education is very different from that of pastors, the pastors are amply prepared to provide the spiritual support and biblical guidance that victims need for their survival and recovery from damages caused by the abuse. Collaboration works well when caring for victims as well as abusers.

G renz
It is essential for church leaders to recognize the importance of upholding the individual's dignity and worth. At times, however, we as church leaders do not do this, when we remain silent on the issue of domestic violence. Our silence might contribute to victims' feeling isolated and devalued. I remember when our church's Care Ministry Coordinator, Judy, (a social worker by trade) approached me early one fall and stated, "October is domestic violence awareness month. You need to do a sermon that addresses domestic violence." My initial response was that this issue does not need to be addressed from the pulpit, but as we dialogued I sensed some conviction (I believe by the Holy Spirit, not by Judy) that I should no longer be silent about domestic violence. As I searched the Bible, I discovered a number of chapters in Psalms that would apply to someone experiencing such abuse. It is out of that study that I developed a sermon on Psalm 143 for our Domestic Violence Awareness Sunday. Below is a sample sermon outline that might be useful for someone interesting in preaching about domestic violence.

Sermon Title: Beaten and Broken
Text: Psalm 143
Introduction
- *Illustration:* Real story of domestic violence (DV)
- What is DV?
- How prevalent is DV? How prevalent is DV among Christians?
- While Christian marriages might have a lower occurrence of abuse, DV occurs in Christian homes as well.
- *Transition:* Psalm 143 can become a prayer of one experiencing DV (it will serve as a framework for the message)

God hears our distress and hurt (vs. 1-4)
- Description of the psalmist's distress and hurt
- DV brings a similar distress and hurt
- Why does DV happen, even in Christian homes?
- Obvious reasons (i.e., the need for control due to low self-esteem; difficulties controlling anger and other strong emotions; feeling inferior to the other partner in education and socioeconomic background; or use of alcohol or other chemical substances)
- Misunderstanding of headship and submission scriptures: explore Ephesians 5:22-23
- God does not condone DV (Prv 6:16-17; Jer 22:7; Ez 18:10-13; 22:7, 27-20; Rom 3:14-17)

God hears our cries for deliverance (vs. 5-12)
- Description of the psalmist's cry for deliverance and the character of God (personal God)
- For victims of DV, we are to call out for deliverance.
- Abuse is not the victim's fault
- *Illustration:* A study of battered Christian women in *Christianity Today* reveals that abused women blame their abuse on their own inability to submit to their husbands.
- You cannot change the abuser.
- God has called His people (the Church) to be a part of deliverance.
- *Illustration:* Negative response of the church—Kiara's story (http://www.hiddenhurt.co.uk/Personal/Kiara.htm)
- We cannot be silent about DV. We need to get involved.

Conclusion:
- Address abusers: Though God is against your actions, He can restore you. Seek out help.
- Address victims: Seek help.
- Our desire is for you to find deliverance.

Albertini
I do hope that more church social workers will speak to their pastors about the need to address domestic violence and in doing so join the global effort to bring greater awareness and healing. Karen's case study is useful for discussing the nature of the problem which victims of domestic violence might face. The story is also useful in delineating the roles of pastors and other professionals. It also helps us to envision how the collaborative approach might work. For instance, one of the social work profession's values calls for advocacy for justice; it is fitting that it includes justice for victims of domestic violence. Another social work value calls for upholding the individual's dignity and worth, while another recognizes the importance of human relationships. Many of the underlying values and beliefs that form the foundation for social work education, practice and policies today trace back to the teachings of the Old and New Testament writings. Our American culture has changed tremendously since the inception of the profession of social work; still the biblical principles and Christian distinctiveness remains and are taught, especially in Christian universities' social work program.[24] Church leaders today have at their disposal Christian social workers, trained to deal with domestic violence as well as many other personal and social problems. Some of those social workers are already working in nearby community agencies with programs designed to help, for example, both victims and abusers involved in domestic violence situations. As with other social problems, more church leaders are encouraged to get involved with existing programs and to help to shape or bolster service delivery systems, especially for victims who could be referred from churches.

Conclusion

Collaboration in pastoral care and social work would be ideal in Janet's case. Domestic violence is definitely one of those problem areas that require immediate attention and action. Violence leaves no room for a wait-and-see mindset. When it comes to domestic violence, delays in services could result in further abuse or even death of the victims and/or the abusers. Care of both victims and perpetrators of domestic violence requires skills and training that are beyond the scope of pastoral care. Therefore, domestic violence merits even closer collaboration between pastors and social workers. Dealing with all the issues we have covered thus far, readers might have gathered that many people are going to pastors for help to deal with almost every type of social problems. Therefore, churches are not considered solely as places of worship but places of refuge. Pastors who are aware of the social problems that affect people's lives and are well-prepared to connect them to appropriate community-based resources are invaluable to those whom they serve.

Sometimes the people who need help are the ones accustomed to helping others, church leaders and their family. How often do we hear the phrase: "*Who really pastors the pastors or counsels their family when they are in crisis?*" In the upcoming chapter, the case study will address needs of Christian leaders and their family. The story also highlights areas where it might be appropriate to utilize a network of Christian social workers who are trained to respond with confidential care to the family, outside of traditional church settings.

CHAPTER 5

Healthy Marriage and Family
Relationships in Ministry

Introduction

As we focus our attention on challenges faced by leaders and their families who are active in ministry, it is befitting to open this chapter with a story about the famous Graham family. As many will attest, it takes hard work and commitment to develop and maintain healthy marriages and family relationships while serving in ministry. We want readers to consider the advice given by Billy Graham in an interview published by Terry Muck and Harold Myra in Christianity Today. The interview was first published in the November 18, 1988, Issue. Reporters questioned the seasoned preacher about safeguards he and his family had put in place over the years to help him maintain spiritual purity and deal with other family-and-ministry-related issues. Graham's response showed direct connections between his efforts to maintain integrity, balance with a healthy family life, and success in ministry. Giving credit to his marriage partner of sixty-three years, Ruth Graham, Graham states:

> Well, first of all, I have a marvelous wife. She reared our children while I traveled. She travels with me most of the time now, at least, because our children are all gone from home. It's good to have her with me. Also, as a young man I heard about two or three classic examples of moral failure. One was an official of a Christian school. It was frightening to see how quickly a man's ministry could be destroyed that way. Those were object lessons the Lord allowed me to see to warn me. I decided there were three areas that Satan could attack in—pride, morals, and finances. Over the years, I tried to set up safeguards against the dangers of each. . . . From the earliest days; I've never had a meal alone

with a woman other than Ruth, not even in a restaurant. I've never ridden in an automobile alone with a woman.[1]

In addition to Graham's story, we would like our readers to consider the case study below, which we hope sheds some light on some of the challenges families might face in ministry.

Case Study: Ministry with Two of a Kind

◘Sam and Sara Johnson have been traveling together as evangelists ever since they got married in their mid-twenties. In fact, until little over three years ago, the couple spent most months out of the year teaching the gospel in remote parts of the world. Sara's primary role was to organize and work out details of their trips. Upon their arrival in a foreign land, it was usually her responsibility to help to organize local talents and lead the singing and worship portion of services before each of the sermons, presented by Sam. Depending on the nature of the engagement and culture, Sara also conducted workshops for women and other groups in local churches or communities. Sam and Sara were always very passionate about spreading the gospel of Jesus Christ. Each understood and supported the other's role in ministry. Even though they had many private discussions about what they would do when the time came for them to have children, they were not fully prepared for the extent of changes that took place once Sara became pregnant. Due to some medical complications, she had to return home to the U.S. earlier than expected, leaving Tom alone to continue the traveling ministry.

Sara discovered within three months that she was carrying not just one baby but a set of twins. She also developed pregnancy-related diabetes, placing her and the babies at medical high risk. In order to address the medical complications, a decision was reached for her to return home to the U.S. to participate in strategic prenatal care for high-risk pregnancies. That decision turned out to be a good one because seven and a half months into her pregnancy, Sara' mother rushed her to the hospital to deliver two premature baby boys by Caesarean section. Sam, unfortunately, was still wrapping up his preaching engagements in Asia and was unable to make it back in time to be by her side. Due to their premature births, the babies remained in the neonatal care unit of the hospital for five extra weeks until each was cleared for release. Once both boys were home, Sam and Sara decided that it was best for her and the babies to remain state-side where they could have easy access to ongoing medical care. With the family settled, Sam gradually resumed his evangelistic ministry overseas; however, it would never again be the same as when he and Sara ministered side-by-side.

Life as they knew it changed drastically. They were now a family of four living just as much time together as apart. Sara's absence in ministry meant that

Sam had to make all the arrangements for the trips and rely more on local talents in the places he visited to conduct the worship services. Though Sam experienced delight in seeing God at work in his ministry, he also experienced loneliness on the road and missed Sara and the boys terribly. For Sara the new life meant raising the boys mostly on her own, which presented some challenges for her. Although she was very excited about motherhood, nothing prepared for her for life as a single mother. Often she found herself having to make family decisions without the benefits of consulting with Sam. For instance, she had to make many decisions related to family's finances, the boys' health care and general household issues. In some rare cases, she was able to get hold of Sam by cellphone or some form of internet connection, but more often, he was out of reach, leaving her to make decisions on her own. Sara also experienced loneliness due to Sam's absence. Within a year of Sam's traveling solo, he and Sara realized that both were developing a habit of purposefully distancing themselves emotionally in order to cope with frequently having to separate and say goodbye.

With Sam gone for weeks at a time, their relationship had to change, especially as it related to intimacy. Prior to the change, Sam and Sara viewed themselves as each other's best friend. They were affectionate and inseparable, both at home and abroad. They enjoyed spending long hours talking about their experiences in ministry, their hopes and dreams. It was quite the norm for them to plan and take romantic get-a-ways. Now it all seemed like a lifetime away. Nothing had prepared them for the struggles each faced in trying to maintain healthy lives separated by ministry. To the world outside, even their close friends, they appeared happy; they put on a good front, but in the privacy of their home, they were struggling to maintain a healthy marriage and family life. Their desire is to develop a healthy family life while remaining committed to ministry but with no one to confide in, they struggle in silence. They keep telling themselves that God's grace is sufficient.

Theological Reflections: Ministry near or far?

"But you, keep your head in all situations, endure hardship, do the work of an evangelist, discharge all the duties of your ministry."
2 Timothy 4:5

Ministering couples experience both the joys of ministry and the stress that often accompanies ministry. A survey of clergy couples conducted by David and Vera Mace revealed various satisfying and dissatisfying factors concerning ministry. The top five satisfying factors are shared Christian commitment, unity of purpose, nurturing support from the congregation, high status/respect in community, and wife's close identification with husband's work. The top five dissatisfying factors are marriage expected to be model of perfection, time pressures due to husband's busy schedule, lack of privacy, financial stress, and no in-depth sharing with other church couples.[2] This survey illustrates the regular struggle of ministry couples who are passionate about serving God, yet experience various frustrating and stressful byproducts of ministry.

Reflecting on our case study in this chapter, at first we seemed to find conflicting biblical statements in the New Testament about ministry and marriage. Jesus teaches his followers to put nothing or no one before their service to him, including one's family (Mt 10:34-39). Paul writes that is it not good for a man to marry (1 Cor 7:1) because he cannot fully focus on the affairs of the Lord (1 Cor 7:32). Paul writes that it is good for a man to remain single to maintain focus on the affairs of the Lord. Conversely, Paul describes married men and women as people distracted by the world (1 Cor 7:33-36). However, there are biblical texts that affirm marriage.

The author of Hebrews instructs readers that "Marriage should be honored by all, and the marriage bed kept pure, for God will judge the adulterer and all the sexually immoral" (Heb 13:4). "As a community, believers must respect marriage as the gift of God and support those who share the marriage relationship with empathy and affection."[3] In his instructions to Timothy about false teachers, Paul states that forbidding marriage is theologically wrong, because God created marriage as something we are to participate in with thanksgiving.[4]

Though these texts might seem conflicting, they are actually very helpful in forming a well-rounded understanding of marriage and ministry. First, we need to understand that Jesus was not dismissing the domain of family relationships, but he was stating that the disciples and those who come to believe the message of Jesus would not only be widely hated; even their own family would reject them.[5] Therefore, when it comes to salvation and following Jesus, there will be family difficulties from those members who do not believe.

Second, marriage is something that has great value. As a relationship created by God (Gn 2:18), extending out of the relational character of God, marriage is good because everything God created he labeled as "good." Therefore, no one should instruct others that marriage should be rejected as ungodly or evil. For those in full-time ministry, pursuing marriage is something that is not wrong. Third, though marriage is good, marriage can heighten or add stress in our ministry and vice versa. Such stress is what Paul is discussing in 1 Corinthians 7. Examination of the context of these verses indicates that Paul is making a general statement here (1 Cor 7:25). "Clearly his [the married man's] time is divided between pleasing his wife and children, and the Lord—marriage places additional obligations on him. The unmarried woman is no different in her calling ..."[6] Paul acknowledges that marriage will bring a level of difficulty and stress to one's ministry; however, later in this letter he is clearly suggesting that it does not disqualify one from ministry (1 Cor 9:5). It is obvious that the needs of family and ministry can easily create tension within a marriage.

Fourth, when making life and ministry decisions, married couples should first consider the family, with ministry taking a secondary position. In his instructions about church leaders in 1 Timothy and Titus,[7] Paul states that if a leader has a family he is to manage the children. "The pastor should be the head of the household, and he should have his children under control. This does not mean that the pastor's children should not be allowed to be children! It means that they are to respect the Lord and their parents and grow to be examples as all Christians should."[8] Eli's leadership of his sons illustrates the consequences of not following this principle. He had no control over his two sons, Phinehas and Hophni, who took meat from sacrificial animals before they were dedicated to God and had inappropriate relationships with women. God pronounced doom on Eli because of his failure to discipline his sons (1 Sm 2:22-36). Even though Eli was effective in ministry, God also expected him to address his family problems. Before couples can lead effectively in ministries they need to be able to lead their family well; therefore, family needs to be top priority in their decision-making.

The tension in balancing family and ministry can be overwhelming for couples. Yet, we are told that God's grace is sufficient for us to navigate through the struggles (1 Cor 12:8; 1 Pt 1:3). In addition, as ministering couples experience struggles and stress they can call upon God for wisdom and have the promise of receiving his wisdom (Jas 1:2-5). The tension between family and ministry can easily overpower them when they try to manage in their own strength. At times ministry couples do not rely on God for strength, wisdom, and help. There is a danger of developing what might be called a messiah complex, believing that if they do not "do" the ministry, no one will (might be even thinking no one else can). This is a form of pride, thinking that God cannot continue the ministry without us. The Bible clearly states those who are proud will be humbled (Is 2:17-18). When the Corinthian church was divided over human leaders, Paul directed the church to move away from the perspective that it is through human effort that church growth happens (1 Cor 3:1-15). "God is the source of the growth; no man can take the credit. Furthermore, no one man can do all the necessary work. Paul planted the seed, Apollos watered it, but only God could make it grow."[9] We need to recognize that the ministry can go on without us; however, no one else is called to assume responsibility for his family as long as he is capable of doing so.

Before concluding this section, it is important to mention a crucial biblical principle related to this topic. Effective couples in ministry need to listen keenly to God. Isaiah says, "This is what the LORD says—your Redeemer, the Holy One of Israel: 'I am the LORD your God, who teaches you what is best for you, who directs you in the way you should go. If only you had paid attention to my commands, your peace would have been like a river, your righteousness like the waves of the sea.'"[10] It's difficult to know how God wants us to navigate the tension between ministry and family unless we take consistent time to listen to God's voice through the study of the Scriptures and prayer. To live in this way is a special challenge, because it is so easy to be superficial. We are so busy! We have so many urgent things to do, so many people to meet, so many events to attend. Families require a lot of time and energy in order to remain healthy. With all that is vying for our attention, the greatest need is to make space for God to speak. Jesus was a very busy person, even to the point of missing meals (Mk 6:31). Jesus was rarely left alone. Therefore, he had to make time to be alone, to give undivided attention to God, and to pray.[11] Those times must have given him awareness of God's sovereignty, of his own identity, of his mission, and of his relationship with the Father. If Jesus needed such solitude for listening to God, certainly we do!

Reality Dialogue Questions

Did Sam make the correct decision in choosing to return overseas? Is it possible for this ministering couple to fulfill a calling to this specific type of ministry?

In ministry as in life, some decisions require little to no forethought, but others require deep soul-searching and wise counsel. Sam's decision fits with the latter. As a spouse or parent, one's decision to leave the family for extended periods or repeatedly requires careful thought and consideration about God's principles concerning both family and ministry. Sam's decision unfortunately resulted in a serious void in this family. There is no one else on earth, as long as he remains alive, with the calling to be a husband to his wife or a father to his children. His extended absences from the home mean that he was not available to be the father or husband the family needed.

Sam and Sally understand their calling as international evangelists. As one examines the case study, their strategy of fulfilling their calling is traveling overseas for extended periods, holding evangelistic events. The answer to the question above is "yes." Sam and Sally can still fulfill their calling as international evangelists, but the key will be for them to adjust their strategy, at least for a season. They can still be international evangelists at home in North America. With globalization, the world is shrinking and coming to us. There is a growing need for evangelists among many ethnic communities that surround our churches, especially in large cities. Assuming that they have a sponsoring church, Sam and Sally can fulfill their calling locally by reaching out to the ethnic communities around their church until their children and family develop to a point where they can resume traveling overseas. They would still be fulfilling their calling by adjusting their strategy.

Synergistic Dialogues: Principles to Build on

"If you serve, do so with the strength God provides, so that in all
things God may be praised through Jesus Christ."
I Peter 4:11

G renz
Traveling evangelists are not the only church leaders who experience the types of tension between family and ministry described in the case study. In addition, many church leaders struggle with issues related to intimacy, stress and burnout, personal and sexual boundaries, power management, and/or spiritual vitality. Moreover, many of these issues are interrelated, like family life and stress management. For example, as church leaders, we can make our homes a place of rejuvenation. For me, I experience rejuvenation with my family through play. I find refreshment as I play games with my wife and children or play in the pool. Sometimes I am tired, so I have to decide intentionally to play a game, knowing that this activity will reenergize me. We also enjoy watching movies together as a way to relax and be refreshed. For each of us, we need to find those activities that rejuvenate us. We must be careful not to let too many activities pull us away from the family. Most of us already spend too much time away from our families, so it is best to find some activities around or in our homes. For some people it might be gardening, fixing up cars, or painting. For others, doing crafts, boating, cycling with one's spouse and/or children might be the thing. Some of the problems affecting families in ministry can be handled through intentional personal discipline and habits; however, there are times when church leaders need help from others. Often I think of accountability groups consisting of other church leaders that can help us navigate through some of our struggles. However, what about those issues that we feel that no one in our church or other churches can help us with? Sometimes there is a need for a safe space to go to get help with our struggles, but we might be unsure where to find such a place .

A lbertini
How true! It is often a struggle for ministering families, especially in our fast-paced society, to find time to do the things that allow them to grow and de-velop health family bonds. Such problems are not unique to families in ministry. Yet, there does seem to be some added stress for ministering families. Leaders in the church in particular might not be accessing resources such as counseling to help them to cope with stressors related to ministry. It is not so easy to—as you say—find that safe place to turn to for help. Family and marriage counseling for those serving in ministry is another area where the collaborative approach might prove helpful. A Christian social worker with a background in individual and family counseling would be a great resource for church leaders and their

families. With a network of such service providers in the community, safe and confidential service might be readily available to ministers outside the church setting. Much work is needed to remove the stigma that is often placed on Christian leaders who find themselves in need of professional care. If more church leaders were to speak publicly about the benefits of professional counseling or restorative care for ministers and their families, perhaps such stigma would be reduced.

Conclusion

This chapter addressed important questions concerning direct care for pastors and their families. It is suggested that pastors and their families stand to benefit from the creation of a specialized network of Christian social workers who possess expertise in family counseling, and who are able to provide confidential services away from the leaders' church environment. We do, however, offer this caveat, that such networks of counselors be extensive enough so that no social worker ever counsels his or her own church leaders or their families. That is, we do not propose that social workers should provide professional counseling to their own pastors. Such relationships would not be in alignment with the ethical standards of the profession of social work that proscribes "dual-relationships."[12]

The upcoming chapter highlights the work of many Christian organizations, which we argue are taking the work of the church well beyond the wall of the sanctuary.

CHAPTER 6

Traditional Approaches to Social Ministries

Introduction

Unlike Chapter Two, where readers were asked to locate the "church of Jesus Christ," this chapter focuses on characteristics and the role of the church. It includes symbolism from Scriptures that depict the church with a feminine persona. The Scriptures call the church to a mission that requires her to respond with mercy and love to people and communities. Here are some of the attributes of the church that are provided in the Bible:

She is a part of a profound mystery of God (Eph 5:32)
She is the pillar-foundation of truth (1 Tm 3:5)
She is the Body of Christ (Col 1:24)
She is God's household (Eph 2:19; 1 Tm 3:5)
She is a model to be imitated (1 Thes 2:14)
She witnesses with authority (Act. 1:18)
She is loved by Christ (Eph 5:25)
She is built by Christ to live in victory (Mt 16:18)
She is appointed overseers by God (Acts 20:28)
She is like a bride adorned for her wedding (Rv 19:7)
She is under Christ's authority (Eph 1:22)
She is welcoming (Acts 15:14)
She embodies diversity (Mt 28:19)
She sends out workers (Acts 15:3)
She seeks out the needy and helps them (1 Tm 5:16)
She is vulnerable to division (1 Cor 11:18)
She is able to stumble (1 Cor 10:32)
She is a place for healing (Jas 5:14)
She provides judgments concerning believers (1 Cor 5:12)

All of the above attributes are useful in examining how religious organizations in the U.S. might associate their work with the mission and attributes of the church.[1] This information is also useful when considering how nationally-known Christian organizations associate their work with the role of the church.

Examples of Christian Social Ministry Organizations

Instead of presenting the usual case study following this introductory section as is the case in all preceding chapters, this chapter opens with a discussion of U.S.-based Christian organizations described in no particular order of priority or ranking. Our aim is not to provide an exhaustive study of the organizations since more detailed information about each organization is available on its websites and other independent sources, such as newspaper articles and reports. We will, however, examine the various organizations' missions to determine whether connections exist between their missions and that of "the church." Several of the organizations we discuss are reporting significant increases in the numbers of people to whom they are providing services.

For instance, Catholic Charities, which serve one in eight of the people living in poverty in the U.S., noted a ten percent increase in those requesting services beginning in 2008. Feeding America also noticed a marked increase, thirty percent, in people needing assistance to secure food in 2008.[2] As the need for faith-based or Christian social ministry services increases, it become even more important to understand how such organizations are navigating their way through society while maintaining focus on the Biblical mandates for the church.

Before discussing the various Christian organizations any further, we would like to define two terms that are often used to describe such organizations: parachurch and faith-based organization. One possible definition of a parachurch is an organization which exists alongside the church, parallel to the church, whose functions and goals and membership might overlap with that of the church.[3] Nathan Baker highlights several characteristics of a parachurch that are worth noting:

> 1) Often they are led through entrepreneurship leaders who gather a constituency; 2) typically they gather financial support from members of key churches and or denominations; 3) most are unconcerned and/or unaccountable to the procedures and structures of denominations; 4) most have a strong evangelistic zeal of making converts; 5) some are judgmental of established churches; and 6) most are single-issue groups(i.e., Bible distribution, world and local hunger, family concerns, teenage drug addiction).[4]

The term "faith-based organization" is more inclusive than "parachurch." The 2003 AmeriCorps Guidance defines a faith-based organization as:

- a religious congregation (church, mosque, synagogue, or temple)
- an organization, program, or project sponsored/hosted by a religious congregation (might be incorporated or not incorporated)
- a nonprofit organization founded by a religious congregation or religiously-motivated incorporators and board members that clearly states in its name, incorporation, or mission statement that it is a religiously motivated institution
- a collaboration of organizations that clearly and explicitly includes organizations from the previously described categories.[5]

As stated above, faith-based organizations include churches and parachurch organizations; however, the key to faith-based organizations is the connection to a religious community. Let us consider, for instance, the work of the well-know organization called Teen Challenge. The aim here is to see whether the organization's mission relates to the Great Commission. Teen Challenge got its start in 1959 in Brooklyn, New York, by the Reverend David Wilkerson. The history of the organization and Wilkerson's work is captured in the popular book entitled The Cross and the Switchblade. According to the organization's website, its mission is to provide youth, adults and families with an effective and comprehensive Christian faith-based solution to life-controlling drug and alcohol problems in order to become productive members of society. By applying biblical principles, Teen Challenge endeavors to help people become mentally sound, emotionally balanced, socially adjusted, physically well, and spiritually alive. Teen Challenge's mission statement connects with the Great Commission in that it employs a Christian faith-based solution to people affected by life-controlling drug and alcohol problems and teaches them to apply biblical principles as described in Matthew 28:18-20, where Jesus instructs his followers to help people of all nations to apply Biblical principles to their lives: "All authority in heaven and on earth has been given to me. Therefore go and make disciples of all nations, baptizing them in the name of the Father and of the Son and of the Holy Spirit, and teaching them to obey everything I have commanded you."[6] Based on the characteristics of the church (she embodies diversity, sends out workers, and seeks those truly needy and helps them), Teen Challenge's mission is commensurate with "the church's" mission depicted in the Great Commission.

Next, consider this listing of some of the Christian organizations that mobilized to provide valuable services to people and communities affected by the disaster that resulted from the September 11th attacks. Also, compare for yourself the missions of some of these organizations on the list as was done with Teen Challenge above.

Religious Responders to the September 11th Disaster

American Baptist Men's Ministries	Christian Disaster Response
Catholic Charities USA	Church of the Brethren
Church World Service	Lutheran Disaster Response
Episcopal Relief and Development	Nazarene Disaster Response
Mennonite Disaster Service	Southern Baptist Disaster Relief
Presbyterian Disaster Assistance	United Jewish Communities
The Salvation Army	United Methodist Committee on Relief

Southern Baptist Convention (SBC)

SBC created in 1845 in Augusta, Georgia. In 1997, the SBC created the North American Mission Board (NAMB), with the distinct purpose of assisting Southern Baptists in their task of fulfilling the Great Commission in the United States, Canada and their territories. Their strategy involves sharing Christ, starting churches and sending missionaries. SBC's primary charge to NAMB is embodied in these nine areas: 1) Appointment and Support of Missionaries; 2) Evangelism; 3) Establishment of New Congregations; 4) Christian Social Ministries; 5) Volunteer Missions; 6) Missions and Missions Education; 7) Communicating the Gospel Through Technology; 8) Strengthening Associations; and 9) Disaster Relief.[7]

Catholic Charities

This organization's history dates back to the early 1700s when French Ursuline Sisters opened an orphanage in New Orleans. By the mid-1800s, the demand for Catholic charities increased dramatically. In the early 20th century, a Catholic Charities network had developed to provide social services and health care and serve as an advocate for the poor. The mission of Catholic Charities is to provide service to people in need, to advocate for justice in social structures, and to call the entire church and other people of good will to do the same. Catholic Charities USA is the national office for over 1,700 local Catholic Charities agencies and institutions nationwide. Catholic Charities USA provides strong leadership and support to enhance the work of local agencies in their efforts to reduce poverty, support families, and empower communities. Catholic Charities USA's members provide help and create hope for more than 8.5 million people of all faiths each year. Today Catholic Charities serves people living in poverty and has a strong voice conveying expertise on most poverty and social welfare issues as well as matters relating to disaster.[8] In February 2009, President Barack Obama appointed Father Larry Snyder, President of Catholic Charities USA, to the President's Council of Faith-based and Neighborhood Partnerships. The Council advises the new office and offers advice on policy issues to the President. Father Snyder will work with the staff of the Oval Office and 24 other religious and community leaders of diverse political, religious, and community backgrounds from across the country.[9]

International Justice Mission (IJM)
IJM founded as a faith-based organization in1997, employs investigators, law-yers and social workers who intervene in partnership state and local authorities in individual cases of abuse ensure proper support for the victim of abuse and appropriate action against perpetrators. IJM seeks to make public justice systems work for victims of abuse and oppression who urgently need the protection of the law. "In the tradition of abolitionist William Wilberforce and transforma-tional leaders like Mother Theresa and Martin Luther King, Jr., IJM's work is founded on the Christian call to justice articulated in the Bible (Isaiah 1:17): Seek justice, protect the oppressed, defend the orphan, plead for the widow."[10]

In addressing violence, IJM reports that it has fully integrated the role of social workers and capitalized on their expertise in addressing domestic and other forms of violence against women and others. Readers should bear in mind that IJM's model is different from the model proposed in this book. However, it is important to note how IJM designed its model to promote collaborations be-tween IJM's investigators, lawyers and social workers as they intervene in cases of abuse and in partnership with state and local authorities.[11] IJM indicates that:

> "By pushing individual cases of abuse through the justice system from the in-vestigative stage to the prosecutorial stage . . . in all of its casework, IJM has a four-fold purpose: 1) Victim Relief—IJM's first priority in its casework is im-mediate relief for the victim of the abuse being committed. 2) Perpetrator Ac-countability- IJM seeks to hold perpetrators accountable for their abuse in their local justice systems. Accountability changes the fear equation: When would-be perpetrators are rightly afraid of the consequences of their abuse, the vulner-able do not need to fear them. 3) Victim Aftercare-IJM aftercare staff and trusted local aftercare partners work to ensure that victims of oppression are equipped to rebuild their lives and respond to the complex emotional and phys-ical needs that are often the result of abuse. 4) Structural Transformation -IJM seeks to prevent abuse from being committed against others at risk by streng-thening the community factors and local judicial systems that will deter poten-tial oppressors." [12]

The Salvation Army
The Salvation Army in the U.S. traces its history to 1880 when Commissioner George Scott Raiton and seven women officers arrived at Battery Park in New York City. Despite much religious persecution, Railton and other Salvationists developed the organizations in other states. Today the Salvation Army continues as an international movement, and an evangelical part of the universal Christian Church. Its message is based on Scriptures. Its mission is to preach the gospel of Jesus Christ and to meet human needs in His name without discrimination; for instance, the organization provided one-on-one social-service-related case man-agement to help victims of September 11th.[13]

Theological Reflections: Church without walls

"Religion that God...accepts as pure and faultless is this: look af-
ter orphans and widows in their distress and...to keep one's self
from being polluted by the world."
James 1:27

The organizations above have greatly influenced our society by representing the grace and mercy of Jesus Christ as they provide social services. Yet, some tensions exit between some churches and parachurch organizations. At times, there has been a competitive nature to the relationships, as well as a judgmental attitude on the part of both parties. Some church leaders have called into question the legitimacy of parachurch organizations, especially from a theological perspective. A task force of the Lausanne Committee of World Evangelization describes this tension: "A few churches feel they must reject the validity of all groupings other than traditional congregational structures. At the opposite end of the spectrum are those who advocate acceptance of these other Christian ministries not merely as biblically valid, but as equally 'church' in the congregational sense."[14] This tension seems to have created a gap between church leaders and leaders of parachurch organizations. The issue really centers on the relationship between the church and parachurch organizations. In this section, we will address this relationship.

A good place to begin this discussion is to develop a brief description of the Kingdom of God. While this concept is present in the Old Testament, the major source for the Christian conception of the Kingdom of God lies in the New Testament teachings. The following is a summary of affirmations about the Kingdom of God. The Kingdom of God is not a geographic territory, but is God's absolute reign (Mt 18:1-4). God has the right to rule over all creation because he created everything (Jer 16:10).This kingdom is Christ-centered (Mt 25:31ff; Acts 2:36; Eph 5:5). Jesus is not just the herald of the coming kingdom; he is the inaugurator of the kingdom.[15] This kingdom is a present reality (Mt 12:28), yet it a future blessing (1 Cor 15:50).This kingdom belongs also to the followers of Jesus, who receive salvation and eternal life and who become citizens of the kingdom (Rv 5:20; 22:5). With citizenship comes the responsibility to follow and live out the principles and values of the kingdom (Mt 5:20; 7:21; 18:3; 19:23; 23:23; 1 Pt 2:9)."The gospel of the kingdom must be proclaimed to every people, tribe, tongue and nation, so that all people have the opportunity to glorify God and get to know the plan of salvation. Through the proclamation of the kingdom its principles and values will also be spread (Acts 8:12; 28:31)."[16] "A proper ecclesiology understands the church within the context of the kingdom because the biblical concept of the kingdom of God is broader than the church."[17] The church is a product of the kingdom, as well as an agent of the kingdom in the world (1 Pt 2:9).

Even though all of the affirmations are salient, two have important implications for this discussion. The first is that the kingdom of God refers to God's sovereign reign over creation and the second is that the church is an agent of the kingdom in the world. Together we see that the kingdom is a present reality as God's reign is proclaimed and received. We will come back to this idea when we conclude this discussion.

Next, it is important for us to explore the nature of the church. Again, this will be brief, but we will discuss the main affirmations about the church. The first key affirmation is that the church is not a building, but a covenant community of persons who have declared their loyalty to God through Christ. This means that "we share a common allegiance to Jesus which is our highest loyalty [and] we also share a commitment to join together to be the people of God."[18] The implication of this is that we can continue to be the church beyond the walls of a building.

The next affirmation important to this discussion relates to the mandate of the church as a covenanting community. The church has been given a threefold mandate: worship (Heb 10:25; 1 Cor 14:26), mutual edification (Jn 13:12-17; Eph 4:11-13), and outreach to the world (Mt 28:19-20; Mk 16:15). For the purpose of this discussion, we will only focus on outreach. "Our task, however, is not limited to the expansion of the church's boundaries. Rather, it includes sacrificial ministry to people in need. Outreach, therefore, entails service."[19] Jesus did not describe his task as only proclamation, but as proclamation in the context of service (Lk 4:18-19). Our service to those in need is an extension of the mission of Jesus. In addition, evangelism and service together provide a complete concept of the gospel. "It [the gospel] focuses on reconciliation with God, of course. But reconciliation is a social reality, for we are in right standing with God only as we are likewise being brought into right relationship with others."[20] Again, the implication of this is that we can be the church beyond the walls of a building.

The final affirmation is the concept of the priesthood of all believers. The New Testament refers to believers in Jesus as a royal priesthood (1 Pt 2:5, 9), which has implications on our relationship not only with God, but with the world. As priests, we represent Jesus Christ to others in both character and action. To enable us to fulfill this role, Christ gave us spiritual gifts (1 Cor 12:8-28; Rom 12:6-8; Eph 4:11). However, the priesthood of all believers is not a singular concept (i.e., not the priesthood of the believer), but it is a corporate concept. Therefore, it is together that we represent Christ and fulfill the mandate of Christ. Similar to the previous affirmations, the implication is that wherever we are, whether in the church building or outside of it, we are called and enabled to represent Christ to the world.

As we synthesize these affirmations, we would like to conclude that the relationship between the church and parachurch organizations needs to be much more contiguous. A parachurch organization is not the church in its fullness, but it's a part of the church. Related to the kingdom of God, a parachurch participates in kingdom work as it proclaims God's reign, especially when addressing injustice. Such organizations also help fulfill the church's mandate of outreach in service. However, the strongest support for viewing parachurch organizations under the umbrella of the church lies in the priesthood of believers. Jerry White claims, "Whatever ministry a believer performs can and should be claimed as an extension of his local fellowship."[21] Yet, not forgetting the corporate aspect of this concept, "Whatever initiatives an individual or group might believe themselves called by God to make, they should wherever possible seek the counsel, goodwill, support and co-operation of the church. Indeed, they should desire to be a part of the church's work rather than independent of it. They should not be overly hasty in pronouncing it dead, washing their hands of it for they might find themselves sinning against the Body of Christ."[22] The organizations discussed in our case study should not be viewed as separate from the church or as completing ministries. At the same time, these organizations should see themselves as part of the church and seek the wisdom and feedback from other church leaders.

Reality Dialogue Questions

When did parachurch organizations emerge? Is it possible to resolve existing tensions between churches and parachurch organizations?

It is possible to identify Paul as the father of the independent mission agency. However, he was sent by the Antioch church although he seemed not to have taken orders from it. Paul's mission group appears to have autonomy and authority beyond the local church. While the Catholic Church had agencies that seem like parachurch organizations (though some would disagree because they usually operated under the official umbrellas of the institutional church), the rise of parachurch organizations is closely linked to Protestantism. In the U.S., the first parachurch organizations were British mission organizations whose main purpose was the distribution of the Bible during the 18th century. In the mid-19th century, some congregations were partnering with grassroots religious organizations to accomplish various tasks, like publishing, missions, and education. However, this relationship did not last long.[23] Numerous parachurch organizations emerged during this time because of the Second Great Awakening.[24] One of the strongest, longest lasting organizations that appeared during this period was the American Bible Society. However, it was after World War II when the United States experienced an enormous increase of the number and influence of parachurch organizations.[25]

If it is at all possible for churches and parachurch organizations to resolve existing tensions between them, it will only come through the unifying work of God's Spirit and concerted efforts of both entities to unite. The divisions between churches and parachurch organization are not simply self-imposed. In the U.S., all churches and parachurch organizations are expected to function in accordance with the nation's common laws. While operating in compliance with the laws, they receive benefits as well as protections from the government. In order for states to recognize a church or parachurch organization, either must provide proper documentation that includes information about their name, mission statements, organizational structures, and in some cases detailed constitution and by-laws. By its very nature, the process of establishing churches and organizations fosters the separation between the various entities. Churches and parachurch organizations do not operate under the same auspices, partly because the governmental process requires them to make the distinction one from another. Although each organization might operate under different organizational structures, when it comes to the Great Commission, all must operate under the leadership and teachings of Christ. If existing tensions are to be resolved, it will require much more communication and collaboration between churches and parachurch organizations that recognize a biblical mandate to do so.

Synergistic Dialogue: Christ Revealed

"I[Jesus] in them and you in me may they be brought to
complete unity to let the world know that you sent me
and have loved them even as you have loved me."
John 17:7

G renz
Churches and parachurch organizations share the solemn responsibilities of revealing Christ to the world. Organizations identified in this chapter have certainly demonstrated the love of Christ in tangible ways. The key purpose behind all the organizations relates to the idea that by revealing Christ, especially to those who are hurting, key aspects of the Great Commission are realized. John 17:7 addresses the question as to whether churches and parachurch organizations are to work together more collaboratively. If this is any indication, in John, Christ prays for complete unity among His followers: *"May they be brought to complete unity to let the world know that you sent me and have loved them even as you have loved me."* What is essential here is that followers of Christ are recognizable to the world by the unity they display among themselves. When united, they are recognizable as true witnesses of Christ. Often church leaders who become preoccupied with the preaching or proclamation of the gospel do so to

the point of forgetting about the role that unity plays in the revelation of Christ. In John 17, Jesus reminds us that it is through our unity that He is revealed to the world.

Albertini

As a Christian and a social worker, I also see where Christ is revealed in all fights for social justice. If you have heard the saying, "All truth is God's truth," well now, think of all justice as God's justice. Wherever we find people or organizations fighting for justice we know that they are working towards the cause of God; I even include secular organizations. Scriptures are replete with God's concern for justice and the poor. God rewards those who are unified in their work to secure justice and bring aid to the poor, be it in sacred or secular settings. I love the fact that the same Biblical Greek word (δικαιοσύνη) that is use for justice is also used for righteousness.

Grenz

We also have many examples in Old and New Testament communities where God provided models for how society is to be structured or organized to meet the spiritual as well as social needs of people. For instance, in Deuteronomy 15:8-11, see God's instructions: "If there is a poor man among your brothers in any of the towns of the land that the LORD your God is giving you, do not be hardhearted or tightfisted toward your poor brother. Rather be openhanded and freely lend him whatever he needs...Give generously to him and do so without a grudging heart; then because of this the LORD your God will bless you in all your work and in everything you put your hand to. There will always be poor people in the land. Therefore, I command you to be openhanded toward your brothers and toward the poor and needy in your land. Later, in Acts 10:5, more insight is given concerning God's sentiments toward the poor and those who help the poor: "...Your prayers and gifts to the poor have come up as a memorial offering before God." The verse informs that God keeps track of actions taken by individuals and organizations concerned about the poor; in fact, such acts are memorialized.

Albertini

Thinking of all you have said, I see much similarity between the work of parachurch organization, church social work and even key aspects of secular social work, especially in regards to the need to fight for social justice. The need for unity is definitely matched by the enormity of the task.

Conclusion

Careful review of mission statements of all the organizations that were discussed in this chapter revealed crucial information that helps in answering some of the questions raised in this book. For instance, we asked whether we who are in Christian communities are expected to use our social and spiritual gifts to reach out to individuals, families and outside the Christian communities. Are churches to respond positively to the government's call for more engagement in social service delivery? The Christian organizations we studied must have responded affirmatively at some point in their history to such a call. Some might say the organizations responded in line with the popular Nike-slogan—*"Just-do-it."* Based on a review of the organizations' mission statements, they are just doing it. Over the years, many have seized opportunities to serve vulnerable people in the world, and in doing so, they are contextualizing the gospel message. We now direct attention to the next chapter's opening paragraph, which is used to setup the chapter's purpose.

CHAPTER 7

Towards A Collaborative Model: Pastoral Care and Social Work

Introduction

Similar to all the other chapters wherein we addressed particular social issues, this chapter offers readers more opportunities to explore the nature of pastoral care and social work. However, here you will find, for the same reason, a more comprehensive case study that allows readers to revisit some aspects of the issues we covered in the case studies of Chapters One through Five. We find this format helpful in laying the foundation for a deeper understanding of the new Collaborative Model for Pastoral Care and Social Work, which we will develop fully in Chapter Eight. The current case study focuses on works of a well-established pastor name Jethro Moss, who leads in an urban church setting. The case study also includes a team of ministers who work alongside Pastor Moss in providing pastoral care within the church and surrounding communities.

Thus far, we have covered five case studies. We will use the circumstances surrounding each individual and family presented in those case studies which are listed below to illustrate why the church environment that Pastor Moss has created is ideal for synergistic collaboration between pastors and social workers. Let us review the titles of all the previous case studies. By revisiting the case studies' titles, we aim to refresh our readers' memories concerning the social problems and to foster some continuity in thoughts as we move towards the discussion of the collaborative model presented in its entirety in Chapter Eight.

- Chapter One: *Sally and Joseph's Family Crisis*
- Chapter Two: *So Much Homelessness,—What are Pastors to do?*
- Chapter Three: Luke's *Battle with AIDS*

- Chapter Four: *Domestic violence: What if He kills Her?*
- Chapter Five: *Ministry with two of a Kind.*

Each case study will helps us to decipher where some of the boundaries lie between pastoral care ministry and social work in relation to New Testament teachings and social conditions in our society. As we review each case study, readers are encouraged to continue exploring whether the mandate given to the church calls pastors to reach out to all people regardless of spiritual, social, economic or political backgrounds. Readers should also seek to develop for themselves better understandings of the biblical framework for Christian social ministry. Unlike previous chapters, where readers were provided theological reflections right after the topics were introduced, here in Chapter Seven we have deferred such discussions to the next chapter where more in-depth details about the new model for Collaborative Pastoral Care and Social Work are provided.

Case Study: Setting-up the workshop

Christ Community Church

This new case study is about some new developments in pastoral care ministry at a church called Christ Community Church (CCC). CCC is an ideal church setting for new pastors to come and learn about the model for synergic pastoral care. The CCC's pastoral team is comprised of the senior pastor, namely, Moss; five associate pastors and their support staff members; and an energetic set of part-time lay-person volunteers. The team works well together with all members embracing the spiritual principle of synergism taught and promoted by Pastor Moss. At CCC, pastors, staff members and volunteers look to Pastor Moss for Godly leadership. The context of the case study involves the first of a series of workshops that Pastor Moss planned after returning from a conference designed to ameliorate urban church ministries. Here we find that Moss has gathered the entire team plus all members of the church's deacon board. After a group prayer, Pastor Moss began the session by recapping salient information about the conference he attended. He explained that all speakers at the conference provided biblical insights about the "Synergistic Model for Pastoral Care." The focus was on ways by which ministries might be made more effective when pastors develop mutually beneficial collaborations with other faith-based and even some secular organizations in their surrounding communities.

The conference speakers offered to help ministers to develop competencies in creating networks and partnerships in their communities and to improve the provision of spiritual, personal and social care. Conference participants included pastors, evangelists, missionaries, and professional counselors, as well as some faith-based and secular social service providers. The conference presenters were selected based on two criteria—evidence of God's calling upon their lives, and a longstanding history of successfully connecting local churches to the broader community resources. The conference presenters had all published books or articles on the topics. The list also included two professors from Christian universities that have degree programs in church social work. One of the professor's areas of expertise included clinical social work practice, while the other's was "macro" or community practice. Now, the current case study will begin with Pastor Moss' training workshops, which he developed for CCC pastoral team.

The goal of the CCC workshop is to train CCC team members to expand their areas of ministry to include more of the synergistic approaches that Moss learned about at the conference.

Case Study: A Preliminary Workshop on Synergistic Collaboration

◘ After welcoming everyone and explaining the purpose of the workshop, Pastor Moss invited the pastoral team and other participants to use their time together to explore ways of improving how they go about doing ministry in specific areas. Moss explained that each pastor would lead the group's discussions about one of five case studies he provided. After reading and discussing the details of each case, the groups would then develop some ministry goals concerning the people in the case study and identify whether the needs they discovered fell within or outside the purview of pastoral care. With each case study, the five groups were encouraged to "think outside the box" as they developed their goals. The groups also needed to imagine there were no limits to their access to necessary resources to help people who are in need.

Warm-up Exercise

Before the groups begin reading and discussing the case studies, each group was told to take ten minutes to consider a Bible passage taken from Ecclesiastics 10:10. Once they had done so, they were told to find ways to relate that passage to their specific areas of ministry. Each group led by a pastor would then share their views on the passage as it related specifically to their areas of ministry. The discussion below is an example of how such an exercise might be reported once it was completed.

Wisdom Passage: *"If the ax is dull and its edge unsharpened, more strength is needed but skill will bring success."* Ecclesiastics 10:10

Discussant: Pastor Ames, Children's Ministries:
"When we thought about the passage, we found ourselves searching for an idea that the ax might represent. For us, the ax represents everything we employ in ministry—our talents, knowledge and skills. For instance, in children's ministry we have to know a great deal about childhood development and theories about how they learn in order to share the gospel with them effectively. If we are lacking in any of those aspects, represented by the dull ax, then we have to work much harder. With knowledge, we work smarter.

Facilitator: Pastor Moss
How might you acquire such talents, knowledge or skills?

Discussant: Pastor Ames
Well, our group believes that our talents naturally come from God. In school, we learned and developed the knowledge and skills about child development. For instance, working in children's ministry, we have to rely on our talents in teaching God's word, good judgment and knowledge we developed from studying in fields of psychology, social work and education.

Discussant: Pastor Blake, Community Outreach
Our group also thought about the importance of having good skills to counteract the times when there is dullness to the ax. You see, we are convinced that from time to time, with repeated use, the ax will lose its sharpness; that is just reality. Nevertheless, when there is dullness we can still benefit from our skills. We might have to work harder but at least we still have the ax.

Facilitator: Pastor Moss
How did your group relate your ideas to your specific area of ministry?

Discussant: Pastor Blake
We focused on our people-skills. While doing community outreach we have to be skillful in communicating with people in all sorts of places. Sometimes the situation we find ourselves in is not the most ideal. A person we meet, for example, might be having a bad day, and is therefore not welcoming; that is what we mean when we say dealing with a dull ax is a reality. We have to rely on the strength of our people skills to continue to reach out in such a situation.

Discussant: Pastor Cook, Men's Ministries
We also focused on the dullness of the ax, and we talked about the strength that is needed especially when the ax is dull. Working in men's ministry, we see the need to stay strong no matter what. We concentrated on the strength of the one holding the ax and the need to be consistently strong. We talked about the ultimate goal, and successes. Regardless of the condition of the ax, which for us represents resources, we must keep our eye on the goal which is to succeed in meeting our evangelistic goals.

Discussant: Pastor Earl, Missions and International Affairs
One of our team members brought up an interesting question; she asked about the times when the ax is not dull and its edge is sharpened. Does that mean we should apply less of our strength? We decided, no. Regardless of the ministry that we serve in, at home or overseas, we should strive to develop as much skill as possible to do what we do well. We should try to keep our skills up-to-par regardless of the resources available. We all felt that that was wise counsel.

Facilitator: Pastor Moss
This has been a rich discussion on the passage. The discussion provides a good framework for us to begin thinking deeper about each area of ministry. Now proceed to the case studies.

Case Study Exercise: Pastor Moss' Synergistic Workshop

◻**Instructions:** (1) Take about forty-five minutes to read carefully through the entire case study you received and then (2) write a few ministry goals that the group anticipates might be helpful to address the needs of the individual(s) or family as described in the case study. After you have written the group's ministry goals, (3) delineate as many of the type of resources the individual (s) or family might need that you can think of. Once you have made the list, (4) divide the list into two categories, one for the resources that are presently available in the church and the other for the resources that might come from other places outside the church. For example, in reading a case study, if you see the need for emergency surgery or the aid of law enforcement, of course, you would place that need on the list for resources that come from outside the church.

Discussant: Pastor Ames—Case study: *Sally and Joseph's Family Crisis*
Reading the family's story, we were amazed to see the number of problems that were hitting them at once. Yet we all could remember working with some families that had similar experiences. Without God's help and support from other people in such times of crisis, anyone could lose it under such pressure. The two questions provided at the end of the case study really stirred our thoughts: "Do we just wait and see if the family is able to find help?" "Are these needs beyond the scope of pastoral care?" Challenged by the questions, our group decided to seek opportunities to minister to the adults *and* children in the family to the best of our abilities. Therefore, we developed these ministry goals:

Ministry Goals:
1. To offer help to the parents towards finding resources to meet the family's needs that are related to the death of their son.
2. To support the family in their efforts to reach spiritual, psychological, and physical wellness.
3. To help the family to connect with spiritual, psychological and educational resources needed to address challenges the children face.

Church Resources:
1. Pastoral support if desired for funeral service and burial of Joey
2. Pastoral care and support if desired to each family member for spiritual and emotional strengthening
3. Children and young adult program to connect the children socially and spiritually with children in their age range
4. Outreach care for the family (i.e., meals, respite care, or house-cleaning)

Outside Resources:
1. Bereavement care and Funeral Arrangements—Funeral Home
2. Psychological/psychiatric assessments (for Sally)—Professional Counseling Center
3. Medical care (for Sally)—Medical Center
4. Psychological assessment to address anxiety (for Sara)—Professional Counseling Center
5. Professional grief counseling (for the entire family)—Professional Counseling Center
6. Follow-up services/Educational assessment and support services (for John)-School System or Private Educational Assessment Center
7. Tutoring Services/After-school homework assistance (for John)—School system
8. Case management (to assist the family) with coordination of resources from social service agencies
9. Financial Planning/Assessment to address funeral and hospital costs—public or private financial counseling center

Facilitator: Pastor Moss
Pastor Ames and his group have successfully broadened their focus beyond the area of children's ministries to consider the needs of the entire family. They have compiled the list of ministry goals—some that are within the means of the church and other from outside sources. After all groups have presented, we will all discuss the benefits and challenges of collaborating with faith-based as well as secular service providers. Moving on to the next case study, let us focus on Pastor Blake's Group.

Discussant: Pastor Blake—Case study: *Homeless People Sleeping,—What are Pastors to do?*
Unlike the first case study, which highlighted specific needs of individuals within a family who seemed overwhelmed by life's challenges, the case study we just read sheds light on needs of an inner-city church where people who are homeless or under the influence of drugs and alcohol are wandering in off the streets. Instead of a family, the church leader is the one who is overwhelmed by the social problems. Our ministry goals, therefore, are centered on the needs of the broader community.

Ministry Goals:
1. To identify methods of working effectively with others striving to find solutions and address needs of people affected by homelessness, drug abuse and alcoholism.
2. To discover effective ways of responding to homeless people who see the church as a safe place to sleep, and come to bathe or seek food.
3. To explore model programs from inner-city churches with similar social issues, and visions that are further along in their development.
4. To explore how churches with pre-schools evangelize or contextualize the gospel in urban community settings.

Church Resources:
1. The church is already known as a place that offers hope and healing through the gospel.
2. The Pastor's skills and training equip him or her to organize or at least meet with other community leaders who are willing to tackle social problems.
3. The church has access to an ecumenical network of church leaders who might already be working with programs and other groups to combat issues in the community.
4. Church goers usually respect the spiritual guidance and pastoral care that pastors provide.
5. The church is ideally located for some people in need, given that the people are already coming to the church grounds.

Outside Resources:
1. Trained people from community-based shelters for the homeless (free or low cost)
2. Drug and alcohol treatment programs (free or low cost)
3. Experts from the community to conduct awareness workshop concerning the issues
4. Expert case managers from community social service programs
5. Medical treatment centers (free or low cost)

6. Social Services—food, clothing, and hygienic care (free or low cost)
7. Law enforcement to address safety concerns

Facilitator:
As Pastor Blake and his group presented their ideas concerning the need to address problem of homelessness, drugs and alcoholism on the community level, I could not help but relate their ministry goals to this saying of an unknown author, "Past the seeker as he prayed came the crippled and the beggar and the beaten. In addition, seeing them . . . he cried, 'Great God how is it that a loving creator can see such things and yet do nothing about them?' God said, 'I did do something. I made you.'" The group envisions collaborative work that takes the church directly to the community. So, *when homeless people in the community come knocking, do we let them in*? The church goes out offering to help to solve the social ills. We will now look to Pastor Cook and his group for insights into the next case study and their ministry goals.

Discussant: Pastor Cook—Case study: *Luke's Battle with AIDS*
Well, it seems that the challenges confronting the church are expanding even further in this case study. It concerns the problem of HIV/AIDS, which is now not just what a single community or nation faces but is a pandemic across the whole world. The case study zeros in on the troubles of a man who is dying with AIDS, but on top of that, he is talking to his pastor about thoughts of killing himself. His story suggests that he might not be the only person in danger; he has an ex-wife who might unknowingly be at risk. To develop our ministry goals, we decided to focus first on the man, namely, Luke and his individual needs. However, we also saw a need to address HIV/AIDS awareness in the church and even the broader community. We felt that too much is at stake for us to ignore the complexity of the problems that HIV/AIDS presents.

Ministry Goals:
1. To offer immediate help to Luke to get him connected to professional counseling in order to address the mental and medical health issues—especially his suicidal feelings, family issues, loneliness and grief.
2. To provide Luke with loving and supportive pastoral care/counseling that addresses the spiritual questions he is raising in relation to forgiveness, salvation, death and grief-related issues.
3. To develop greater awareness and more education in the church about the nature and effects of HIV/AIDS.
4. To cultivate a church environment that is spiritually and emotionally supportive to individuals and families affected by HIV/AIDS.
5. To increase the church's evangelistic (while maintaining biblical distinctiveness) role in community and even national and worldwide efforts to halt the spread of HIV and tend to those who are suffering.

Church Resources:
1. Pastoral care is available
2. Qualified volunteers might be available in the church to help to increase HIV/AIDS awareness at the church
3. Sermons and teaching on God's grace, mercy and love are available to prepare the church to welcome and support people affected by HIV/AIDS
4. Evangelistic skills are present for faith-based HIV prevention efforts
5. Some denominations which have precedence combating HIV/AIDS are available as models on the local and global levels

Outside Resources:
1. Professional counselor- Community-based Counseling Centers
2. Educators knowledgeable about HIV/AIDS-Public Health Department
3. Medical Care Center
4. HIV/AIDS Educational Resources-films/reading material

Facilitator:
Pastor Cook's group has taken on the AIDS issues with keen attention paid to the personal needs of the man in the case study as well as community needs. They have made it clear that there is a need for more collaboration with professionals in the community as well as a denominational effort around the world. Their presentation reminded me of the adage—"Think globally and act locally." Pastor Earl's group will present the next case study followed by Pastor Doe and his group.

Discussant: Pastor Doe—Case study: *Domestic violence: What if He kills her?*
Our group struggled with the details of Janet's story. It stirred our emotions: frustration, anger, sympathy, fear, and hope. Struck by the reality that anyone's daughter or sister could experience domestic violence, we empathized with the victim. Yet, along with the negative feelings, we were motivated with hope that her visit to the church would be the beginning of a rescue or self-liberation process. We also thought about the needs of the abusers as we listed these ministry goals:

Ministry Goals:
1. To stay available to and supportive to victims like Janet as they make progress toward being safe from domestic violence (DV).
2. To develop greater awareness of the nature of domestic violence among pastoral team and the church (sermons)
3. To learn about resources available for victims and perpetrators of DV.
4. To locate and bolster local shelters for victims of DV.

5. To familiarize pastors with names of counselors who are trained to work with victims of DV.

Church Resources:

1. Pastoral Care available—Janet was aware of it
2. Sermons—DV
3. Church leaders might be able to use their influences to promote   increases in community resources for DV

Outside Resources:

1. Professional Counselor skilled in working with DV
2. Safe-Shelters for victims of DV
3. Local and national material on DV
4. Law Enforcement services

Discussant: Pastor Earl—Case study: *Ministry with Two of a Kind*
There isn't anyone is this room who has served in ministry who has not had to deal with decisions of whether to sacrifice time with his or her family in order to do ministry. It is a fact of life for us. However, sitting here, not directly involved in the situation in the case study and with hindsight, we are able to develop ministry goals related to Sam and Sara, who would be colleagues if they were with us.

Ministry Goals:

1. To develop and promote family enrichment seminars for ministers and their families.
2. To develop a network of professional Christian counselors dedicated to fostering healthy marriage families for ministers.
3. To create opportunities for safe and confidential counseling services outside home church settings by professional Christians.
4. To provide support network for overseas ministers' spouses who remain at home.
5. To develop mentor programs to match younger ministers with more experienced ministers who are sustaining health family relationships.

Church Resources:

1. Church facilities are useful for seminars
2. Mentors are available in the church
3. Pastors are available to facilitate the enrichment seminars

Outside Resources:

Professional Christian counselors in the community—apart from church settings

Facilitator:
Pastors Doe and Earl's groups have put the finishing touches on today's group work. All groups provided ministry goals based on what they anticipate might be helpful to address the needs of the individual(s) or family described in the case studies. The groups also delineated resources which the individual (s) or family might need. They then divided their list into two categories, one for resources already available in the church and another for resources that might come from places outside the church. All of the work completed in today's work shop was done in preparation for the next workshop during which we will brainstorm about actual issues we face in our ministries and develop actual ministry goals for our church. We will also consider what resources are already available here at the church and those that are in the communities around us.

The whole purpose of the "Workshop" case study is to lay the foundation for the new model for PCSW in Chapter Eight. But, before we move on to Chapter Eight to consider details of the model, it is necessary that we solidify the foundation by comparing and contracting the two areas of ministry or work; that way we fully understand distinctions between the roles of pastoral care and social work in context to the church.

Duties in Pastoral Care versus Social Workers

The information about the tasks and responsibilities of each area is derived from the Occupational Information Network (O*NET),[1] a website that was developed under the sponsorship of the US Department of Labor/Employment and Training Administration. The O*NET program is updated periodically. We are using the updated version from 2009. O*NET is one of the nation's primary source of occupational information.[2] The two sets of occupational tasks we have provided are not exhaustive; nor did we intend for the descriptions to cover all ministry or work settings. We are simply providing for readers a general sense of the duties and responsibilities for pastoral care ministers and social workers. The first lists of tasks and responsibilities are what you might see performed in pastoral care ministries. The second list pertains to social workers.

Pastoral Care Tasks

- Pray and promote spirituality
- Read from sacred texts
- Study and interpret religious laws, doctrines, and/or traditions
- Prepare and deliver sermons and other talks

- Organize and lead regular religious services
- Share information about religious issues by writing articles, giving speeches, or teaching
- Instruct people who seek conversion to the Christian faith
- Counsel individuals and groups concerning their spiritual, emotional, and personal needs
- Visit people in homes, hospitals, and prisons to provide them with comfort and support
- Train leaders of church, community, and youth groups
- Conduct special ceremonies such as weddings, funerals, and confirmations
- Administer religious rites or ordinances
- Respond to requests for assistance during emergencies or crises
- Devise ways in which congregation membership can be expanded
- Collaborate with committees and individuals to address financial and administrative issues pertaining to congregations
- Prepare people for participation in religious ceremonies
- Plan and lead religious education programs for their congregations
- Refer people to community support services, psychologists, and/or doctors as necessary
- Participate in fundraising activities to support congregation activities and facilities
- Organize and engage in interfaith, community, civic, educational and recreational activities sponsored by or related to their religion[3]

Social Workers' Tasks

- Conduct interviews with individuals, families, and community-groups
- Complete evaluative assessments to determine problems and needs with consideration for services delivery for various client systems
- Provide individuals, family and groups counseling
- Develop community-based networks to address personal, family and social problems (i.e., mental health, poverty, unemployment, substance abuse and dependence, domestic violence, social adjustment, child care, medical care, job placement, financial and legal counseling
- Provide intervention for students and parents—home and school settings
- Develop and maintain case records and reports
- Counsel parents in need of parenting skills development

- Provide consultation to school personnel address issues related to students' maladaptive behaviors including truancy and other forms of juvenile delinquency
- Consult with law enforcement teams to address legal issues related to child abuse and neglect, or custody arrangements
- Utilize the PCSW Model to develop and review service plans and contracts in consultation with individuals, families or community groups.[4]

Conclusion

Chapter Seven was prepared with the content of Chapter Eight in mind. Readers will find that all the details provided about the conference and the workshops serve to prepare readers to receive the new and synergistic model we plan to introduce fully in Chapter Eight. Here again readers are reminded of the value of developing the types of social service networks described in this book. Such networks will require the investment of time, effort, and wisdom on the part of pastors and social workers; however, the rewards are great. Pastors will discover many helpful partners through this process, but more importantly, the church will be able to expand Christ's message of love, compassion and grace to more people.

CHAPTER 8

Theological Reflections and Model for Collaboration in Pastoral Care Ministry and Social Work

"Let us not become weary in doing good...as we have opportunity, let us do good to all people, especially to those who belong to the family of believers."
Galatians 6:9-10

Albert Einstein commented that "The only reason for time is so that everything doesn't happen at once." With that statement, Einstein highlighted the value of having set rhythms and order to all aspects of life. Knowing the importance of proper timing, we have used all preceding chapters of this book to lay out, sequentially, our call for more synergistic collaborations among people doing pastoral care and social work. It is with confidence in our readers' level of patience and their benevolent spirit that we have embarked upon our literary journey to explore theological and practical reasons for the synergistic approach. We believe that our approach is in alignment with the Great Commission set forth in Matthew 28:16-20. We offer that it is through social and spiritual actions that individuals, families and communities around us come to realize Christ's perfect work of reconciliation, peace, hope, and love.

Today more than ever before, the church is being called upon to increase her level of engagement in social service delivery to poor and hurting people of our society. As she responds to the call, she will find opportunities to extend Christ's message to more people and thereby extend her Christian influence in society. The church is privy to such a great window of opportunity and it comes at a most pivotal time in our nation's history. Christian leaders who contextualize the gospel while addressing pressing social problems will be able to enter directly into places where hurting people live, to share Christ's message of reconciliation, peace, hope, and love.

All Justice is God's Justice

Our primary goal in offering this book is to equip those in Christian ministries who are seeking to go beyond the four walls of the church, to extend services into unfamiliar locales. Using our backgrounds in pastoral care and social work, we have developed a collaborative model that joins those two areas of ministry. Before we present the collaborative model, we find it necessary to undergird it even further with a sound theological foundation. Essential to its foundation is the matter of understanding social service delivery from sacred and secular settings. Some church leaders might wrestle with the idea of believers going outside of the church to secular settings to access social services; for fear that, such resources are inherently antithetical to Christian teachings and are, therefore, to be avoided. In some cases, there might be an element of truth to that notion. Some resources offered in secular settings might involve concepts and techniques that oppose biblical truth; however, a universal rejection of all resources outside the church, based on such fears, lacks a healthy theological perspective. Important to the issue of social service delivery is the principle that God is the source of all justice within the church and beyond the church. The Psalmist confirms this when he declares, "The King is mighty, he loves justice—you have established equity; in Jacob you have done what is just and right" (Ps 99:4). Not only has God established justice, his dwelling is in righteousness and justice (Ps 97:2).

God's presence extends even into just or fair business practices. Solomon writes, "Honest scales and balances are from the LORD; all the weights in the bag are of his making" (Prv 16:11). We see that God is present in all justice, but does God use organizations that make no claims to be Christian to carry out his will for justice? This question leads us to an exploration of God's sovereignty.

God's Sovereignty Seen in Just Acts

The question of whether non-believers are able to carry out God's will is not a new one. While addressing a similar question concerning the actions of people during the first century who were delivering the gospel with wrong motives, the apostle Paul instructed the early church as follows: "It is true that some preach Christ out of envy and rivalry, but others out of good will. The latter do so in love, knowing that I am put here for the defense of the gospel. The former preach Christ out of selfish ambition, not sincerely, supposing that they can stir up trouble for me while I am in chains. Why does it matter? *The important thing is that in every way, whether from false motives or true, Christ is preached.* And because of this I rejoice." (Phil 1:15-18a).

Paul was not saying that he delights in or condones good works done with improper motives, but rejoices in the fact that the gospel is being preached. "The *how* of preaching is not the object of Paul's joy; the *fact* of the preaching is. So it is with just actions; the motives might be wrong but when justice is done, God is glorified. When the Word of God is preached, it overcomes all hindrances and moves on to its goal; its contents are irresistible (Is 55:10–11; 1 Kgs 2:27; 13:2, 5, 9, 17, 32; 2 Kgs 1:17; 9:36; 22:16). The power of the gospel, therefore, does not depend on the character of the messenger."[1] God's sovereign work was also evident in the Old Testament when he used Assyrians, Babylonians, and other non-believing nations to correct the Israelites. Israel as a nation was rebellious towards God, especially seen in unjust acts concerning the poor, widows, and orphans. God used non-believing nations to get Israel's attention and to correct her heart and actions. From this discussion, one can conclude that acts of justice, whether from the church or other social organizations, are sacred acts because of God's sovereign presence in justice, wherever just actions exist.

Another element of this theological foundation for the approach we are about to describe is the collaborative nature of God's community. Ministry resources are not strictly found in the priestly or church leader's domain; though there is a synergy present when such resources are combined. There are two Old Testament examples of collaborative approaches that include the combined efforts of religious leaders and other professionals. The first example occurs prior to the Israelites' entrance into the Promised Land, when God provided instruction for the creation of the tabernacle. God instructed Moses, and "Every skilled woman spun with her hands and brought what she had spun—blue, purple or scarlet yarn or fine linen. And all the women who were willing and had the skill spun the goat hair" (Ex 35:25-26). The second example relates to Solomon's preparation for building the first temple of God. Solomon wrote, "The temple I am going to build will be great, because our God is greater than all other gods... Send me, therefore, a man skilled to work in gold and silver, bronze and iron, and in purple, crimson and blue yarn, and experienced in the art of engraving, to work in Judah and Jerusalem with my skilled workers, whom my father David provided..." (2 Chr 2:5-7). Both of these examples illustrate collaborative efforts that included resources beyond those of the priests responsible for creating a dwelling for God.

Later, in the New Testament, Paul extends ministry beyond the efforts of church leaders, to help his readers see that the mission of the church requires collaborative efforts of people with a variety of gifts, skills, and training. Paul's body metaphor, in 1 Corinthians 12, teaches that there is a need for people with different gifts to meet the needs of the church. Earlier in 1 Corinthians, using a farming metaphor, Paul explains that God has assigned different tasks to various people. Some people will plant seeds of life; others will come along to water the seeds, but God Himself causes the seeds of life to thrive. Neither the ones planting the seeds nor those watering the seeds possess the power to make the seeds grow. After the ones planting and watering the seeds fulfill their respective role, each will receive rewards from God based on his or her efforts (1 Cor 3:1-15). The working relationship between the workers themselves and with God, as described by Paul, is a synergistic one.

Having presented a biblical framework for synergistic collaborations in this chapter as well as in six of the seven preceding ones, we will now focus our attention on delineating the Collaborative Model for Pastoral Care and Social Work. For convenience, we will refer to the Model using the acronym, PCSW. As you examine the PCSW Model, keep in mind its theological foundation. Recognize that God is the source of all justice, whether the acts of justice or corresponding resources originate from a church or other organizations. Moreover, celebrate how God uses all whom he wills for his purpose, from the clergy to the skilled laborer. With the PCSW Model, our intention is to provide an organized and sequenced pattern to enhance the helping relationship and the ways that both pastors and social workers respond to those seeking their help in churches and communities.

Eight Stages of the PCSW Collaborative Model

The PCSW Model is comprised of the eight distinct stages you see outlined below. Each stage, from the first, is connected sequentially, and subsequently each is crucial in the service delivery and helping processes. The stages are interrelated as designed in progressive order for tasks completion. Stage One's tasks are foundational to the ones in Stage Two and so forth through to the eighth stage. Figure 1.0 below shows the foci of the various stages and relates specific tasks that pastors and social workers will endeavor to facilitate as they work together to help individuals, families, organizations, or communities, seeking to accomplish goals that are established during the process. In the left column, you will see each stage chronologically ordered from top to bottom. In the right column, you will find various areas of focus that correspond with progressive developments across the helping relationship. Readers might find it helpful to read through all the tasks accomplished at each stage and then explore the natural progression and connectivity from one stage to another. For instance, see how the tasks at Stage One, with the onset of communication with or about someone in need, naturally lead to the tasks of Stage Two, where information will be gathered in detail. Also, note the value of the information gathered in Stages One and Two, to the tasks completed during Stage Three and beyond.

Figure 1.0: The PCSW Model

Stages	Focus at each Stage of the Pastoral Care and Social Work Model (PCSW)
1	⌈ Collaboration after Initial Contact
2	⌊ Collaboration for Inquiry and Intercession
3	⌈ Collaboration for Strategic Planning and Contracting
4	⌊ Collaboration for Advocacy and Resource Linkage
5	⌈ Collaboration for Transition and Change
6	⌊ Collaboration for Systematic Review of Progress
7	⌈ Collaboration in Making Transition Decisions
8	⌊ Collaboration for Celebration at Closure

The dynamic and complex nature of pastoral care and social work, or of any helping relationships for that matter, precludes us from anticipating the full range of manner in which each person will engage with people who are seeking their help. Nor can any helping model, set on paper, capture completely all the nuances related to the levels of empathy, compassion, and skills that are so vital in developing effective helping relationships. Yet despite such limitations, we have endeavored to delineate the various stages of the PCSW Model. In explaining the Model, we have employed several case studies from previous chapters, with which readers have become familiar, to shed light on the usefulness of the PCSW Model in enhancing Christian ministries. In designing the PCSW Model, our intention is to provide an organized and sequenced pattern to the helping process, to enhance ways with which both pastors and social workers perceive their helping relationships. Each stage of the Model represents a pivotal point at which pastors and social workers might combine their expertise to increase the quality, amount, and types of resources available to people who approach the church for help, and for promoting the spiritual, psychological and social well-being of those served. Each stage allows for distinctions between roles and tasks of pastors and social workers, and offers guidelines for serving individuals, families, organization and communities that seek help to overcome challenges that impede their progress in life. The Model was developed with deep respect and admiration for the role of pastoral care. When applied appropriately, the PCSW Model will enhance pastoral care ministries and social work practices, without detracting from any of the spiritual benefits that motivate people to seek help from pastors in church settings.

Stage One: Collaboration After Initial Contact

Religious organizations are some of the first places that people will go to seek help to overcome life's challenges, once personal and family resources are exhausted. Such is the case in most of the case studies we have covered. Pastors and social workers play key roles in the PCSW Model, designed specifically to enrich pastoral care and social work associated with church-goers. There is an expectation that pastors will most likely be the first persons that people in need turn to for help. Either through telephone calls or visits directly to churches, people will make first contacts with pastors. Once such contacts are made, pastors are the ones who will decide whether it is appropriate to introduce the idea of PCSW collaborations to the individuals, families or communities seeking help. The decision to introduce or initiate the PCSW collaboration process will depend, for example, on the nature of the personal or family problems that are affecting the people whom pastors encounter. From the very first stage of the Model pastors will be presented with opportunities to begin to utilize relevant resources that will become available to those they serve.

For instance, pastors who strive to develop or engage networks of Christian social workers will be at a greater advantage to connect those they serve with needed community-based resources. Therefore, it is important to emphasize precursory actions that must be taken towards developing community and church-based networks that include social workers as key players in the helping process. It is important to understand that the tasks completed subsequent to beginning at Stage One will depend more on efforts of pastors and their church staffs who will develop working relationships with Christian social workers. At Stage One, people will begin to not only share contact information but also to discuss the nature of the problems they face. Pastoral teams who are familiar with social workers in their churches and communities, and who are connected well to networks of resources will be more equipped to employ the PCSW Model. It is very important that pastors understand and convey the message that the PCSW Model is not in any way intended to reduce pastoral involvement or deter those seeking the full benefit of the spiritual guidance inherent to pastoral care. There are several important tasks related to the current stage.

At this stage, pastors and social workers who are contacted by people in need have opportunities to greet and welcome them. It is important to set the tone of the helping relationship with empathy, love and compassion, and at the same time seek preliminary information about the pressing issues. Relevant information such as names, addresses and telephone numbers is also taken at this stage. With the basic information collected, pastors or social workers should then be able to provide information about the benefits of the PCSW process (information package could be provided including list of appropriate service providers from the network).

When necessary, pastors or someone on their staff could assist individuals and families needing to make contact with a specific social worker. While the

PCSW process promotes the use of trained social workers within the church and community networks, it does so in a manner that is complementary to existing resources within pastoral care. In other words, it does not replace pastoral care. Rather it offers people in need the benefits of both pastoral care and social work. Take for example, the case study from Chapter Three, entitled *"Luke's Battle with AIDS: He died before he died"*; in it Pastor Browne was the first person in the church whom Luke chose to confide in about his struggles with AIDS. Aside from spiritual guidance and care, Luke desperately needed mental health counseling to address some of his personal and family issues. Luke also needed other types of social services.

The details of Luke's meeting with his pastor offer some good insight into what constitutes an "initial contact" as described at Stage One of the Model. Another example is in Chapter Seven's case study entitled, *"A Preliminary Workshop on Synergistic Collaboration,"* that lists several "ministry goals" that help to illustrate the importance of, not only the first, but the second stage of the PCSW. For the purpose of review, let us consider "ministry goals" from Chapter Seven. In reviewing, the goals, each reader should think about the task of first stage of the PCSW Model. Consider, for example, how beneficial it would be for Luke if Pastor Browne was able to introduce him to the PCSW Collaborative Model and direct him to a specific social worker, and services within the church and community.

Ministry Goals:
1. To offer immediate help to Luke to get him connected to professional counseling in order to address the mental and medical health issues— especially his suicidal feelings, family issues, loneliness and grief.
2. To provide Luke with loving and supportive pastoral care/counseling that addresses the spiritual questions he is raising in relation to forgiveness, salvation, death and grief-related issues.
3. To develop greater awareness and more education in the church about the nature and effects of HIV/AIDS.
4. To cultivate a church environment that is spiritually and emotionally supportive to individuals and families affected by HIV/AIDS.
5. To increase the church's evangelistic (while maintaining biblical distinctiveness) role in community and even national and worldwide efforts to halt the spread of HIV and tend to those who are suffering.

Church Resources:
1. Pastoral care is available
2. Qualified volunteers might be available in the church to help to increase HIV/AIDS awareness at the church
3. Sermons and teaching on God's grace, mercy and love are available to prepare the church to welcome and support people affected by HIV/AIDS

4. Evangelistic skills are present for faith-based HIV prevention efforts
5. Some denominations which have precedence combating HIV/AIDS are available as models on the local and global levels

Outside Resources:
1. Professional counselor- Community-based Counseling Centers
2. Educators knowledgeable about HIV/AIDS-Public Health Department
3. Medical Care Center
4. HIV/AIDS Educational Resources-films/reading material

Stage Two: Collaboration for Inquiry and Intercession

The PCSW Model is also ideal for helping those who turn to church leaders with expectations that their Christian faith will be ameliorated during their engagement in such helping relationships. For instance, people who go to pastors for help usually expect that as ministers, they will be able to offer prayer and spiritual guidance that is scripturally based. For that reason, the second stage of the PCSW Model depicts a transition process geared towards moving the helping relationship from the first stage to the next. Stage Two includes an important inquiry process that integrates a key element of faith, intercessory prayer. Stage Two distinguishes the PCSW Model from secular helping models. Again, at this stage, it is important to recognize partnerships between pastors and social workers.

To understand the task accomplished during Stage Two, we will focus attention on the "inquiry" component of this stage and then discuss the "intercessory" component in detail. During Stage Two, pastors and their staff may continue the gathering of salient information that allows them to determine the nature of problems presented to them by those who seek their help. Both the pastor and the social worker are bounded by confidentiality guidelines and each is expected to treat people with dignity and respect; those professional skills really come to bear during each stage. While it is not within the purview of pastors to conduct psychosocial and family assessments, they are able at this stage to seek to collaborate with social workers trained to complete such tasks. Some types of assessment reports will naturally remain within the domain of social work. However, with proper release of information procedures and consents from those whom they serve, when appropriate social workers might confer with the referring pastors in order to make proper use of information germane to the success of those whom they serve. Social workers are trained to work with individuals and families and gather information about the personal and family factors, concerning, for instance, depression, suicidal thoughts or domestic violence. Social workers are also able to complete psychosocial, family and community assessments. With the provision of services from social workers, pastors are free to maintain primary focus on spiritual care and guidance.

The manner in which pastors and social workers employ the PCSW Model will contribute greatly to the effectiveness of helping relationships, and to how well those receiving care perceive their chances for success. In the Christian community, it is also well within the norm to expect pastors to use prayer during pastoral counseling sessions. During Stage Two, pastors might also choose to utilize formal or informal spiritual assessment methods to determine the nature of the challenges people face. Consider, for instance, the following assessment questions, which are similar to those George Fitchett provided in his book entitled, Assessing Spiritual Needs: A Guide for Caregivers. 1) What beliefs does the person have, which give meaning to his or her life? 2) What authority does the person use to guide his or her beliefs and spiritual practices? 3) What spiritual practices is the person involved in to support his or her beliefs and relationship with God? [2]

Social workers, on the other hand, might, depending on the circumstances, complete personal and/or family assessments. Consider, for example, the case study from Chapter Two, "So much homelessness: What are pastors to do?" that involves challenges related to people's mental state, experience of homelessness and drugs and alcohol abuse and dependency. Given the complexities of all those issues, we might think about the benefits of having an organized and systematic way (such as the PCSW Model) of helping people in church and community settings. With each stage of the PCSW, it is important to maintain focus on the personhood of each person and the problems that affect their live; as opposed to only focusing on the problems. The PCSW Model is first and foremost people and society-centered, with emphasis placed on its biblical foundations.

Similar to Stage One, during the current stage there are several tasks to be addressed:

- Gather all additional information needed to understand the characteristics of each person, family, or community, the nature of the problems and circumstances that cause people to seek help.
- Convey hope.
- Provide more detailed information about the PCSW Process.
- Include intercessory prayer in the inquiry process when appropriate.

The "intercessory" component is as inherent to the Model as it is to pastoral care. For pastors, it is customary, while providing pastoral care, to include intercessory prayers as a key element in the helping process. Pastors are also equipped with skills to listen, counsel, and encourage those whom they serve. People who turn to pastors for help often will ask them and others in the church to pray with or for them. People who subscribe to the Christian faith view intercessory prayer or prayer on the behalf of others as an effective part of problem solving. Pastors do not only apply intercessory prayer as they engage people; it remains a key component throughout the entire PCSW Model. Therefore, prayer is not only a tool within the helping model; it is also a part of biblically-based intervention strategies. Those who seek pastoral care will often include requests for prayer as part of their plea for help. Although it is well within the purview of pastoral care for ministers to include intercessory prayer across the helping process, that is not always the case for social workers who operate outside church settings. The PCSW offers those seeking help in the church setting a two-pronged approach that allows each discipline to maintain its own ministry and professional boundaries, skills, goals, integrity, values, and hiring practices.

With networks of social workers available to churches, pastors are better able to make referrals to social workers who are able to develop working relationships with people such as those discussed in the case studies covered. Social workers are well-trained to assist people in finding safe places with services to meet their personal, family and social needs. Using elements of the case study below, *"So much homelessness: What are pastors to do?"* from Chapter Seven, let us focus our attention on the list of "outside resources." The "outside resources" are those that are available in community social service organizations.

Ministry Goals:
1. To identify methods of working effectively with others striving to find solutions and address needs of people affected by homelessness, drug abuse and alcoholism.
2. To discover effective ways of responding to homeless people who see the church as a safe place to sleep, and come to bathe or seek food.
3. To explore model programs from inner-city churches with similar social issues, and visions, those are farther along in the developments.
4. To explore how churches with pre-schools evangelize or contextualize the gospel in urban community settings.

Church Resources:
1. The church is already known as a place that offers hope and healing through the gospel.
2. The Pastor's skills and training equip him or her to organize or at least meet with other community leaders who are willing to tackle social problems.
3. The church has access to an ecumenical network of church leaders who might already be working with programs and other groups to combat issues in the community.
4. Church goers usually respect the spiritual guidance and pastoral care that pastors provide.
5. The church is ideally located for some people in need, given that the people are already coming to the church grounds.

Outside Resources:
1. Trained people from community-based shelters for the homeless (free or low cost)
2. Drug and alcohol treatment programs (free or low cost)
3. Experts from the community to conduct awareness workshop concerning the issues
4. Expert case managers from community social service programs
5. Medical treatment centers (free or low cost)
6. Social Services—food, clothing, and hygienic care (free or low cost)
7. Law enforcement to address safety concerns

Stage Three: Collaboration for Strategic Planning and Contracting

People in need who are involved in the PCSW processes stand to benefit not only from the comprehensive "inquiry" and "intercessory" process made available during Stage Two, but also from the carefully developed plans and contracts that address individual, family or community needs at Stage Three. The tasks accomplished in the earlier stages are paramount to the success of those accomplished in the third stage. Whereas in the past, pastors and social workers have worked separately in their respective fields, with the PCSW Model there would be extensive collaboration between them and the people they serve, to develop clear goals and objectives to overcome challenges successfully. As with the preceding stages, it is important to recognize each person's strengths and to obtain their insight into ways to overcome the challenges. Once the individuals, families or communities, with the help of pastors and social workers, have developed the necessary plans and contracts to combat the problems, the next step is to implement the plans. During this stage, it remains important to garner the support of both professionals, with each addressing issues respective to their own discipline.

Take, for example, the case study entitled, *"What if he kills her?"* involving Janet, the victim of domestic violence. In reviewing the corresponding "ministry goals," "church resources" and "outside resources" that were developed in Chapter Seven, the roles of pastors and social workers are illuminated.

Ministry Goals:
1. To stay available to and supportive to Janet as she makes progress towards being safe from domestic violence (DV)
2. To develop greater awareness of the nature of domestic violence among pastoral team and the church (sermons)
3. To learn about resources available for victims and perpetrators of DV
4. To locate local shelters for victims of DV
5. To familiarize pastors with names of counselors who are trained to work with victims of DV

Church Resources:
1. Pastoral Care available-Janet is aware of it
2. Sermons—DV

Outside Resources:
1. Professional Counselor skilled in working with DV
2. Safe-Shelters for victims of DV
3. Local and national material on DV

In Janet's case, it might be necessary to deal immediately with the threat to her safety; therefore, spend time addressing the effects of the abuse and need for safety. In this case, any development of a plan might first require Janet to work very closely with the social worker while keeping the pastor apprised of her progress towards full implementation of the PCSW plan which they collaboratively developed. In other situations, during the planning stage, it might be important to focus more on the personal or family barriers that interfere with spiritual growth and development. One of the benefits of the PCSW Model that really comes through at this stage is that it allows each professional to take appropriate actions to ensure that people's needs are addressed, while at the same time providing opportunities to build continuously on existing resources and creating new networks of resources. It is also at this stage that it becomes clear that in terms of fulfilling the Great Commission, the collaborative approach makes it possible for those seeking services at the church to increase their chances for success in overcoming the challenges.

It is appropriate at this stage to utilize formal plans and contract forms in order to ensure that the helping process is structured. The tasks accomplished at Stage Three include:

- Using all the information gathered during the preceding stages to assist the person(s), family, or community to develop plans that match the agreed upon needs to personal or other types of resources
- Using the plans developed to create working contracts that stipulate the measurable action steps that are needed toward problem-resolutions
- Set time frame for each step on the contract with reasonable completion dates
- Provide more detailed information about the PCSW Process in respect to this stage

Stage Four: Collaboration for Advocacy and Resource Linkage

Some unique opportunities related to the PCSW Model are present at the fourth stage. This stage calls for pastors and social workers to collaborate towards matching people with needed resources, within families, the church and community's network systems. Even though during Stage Three plans are developed to address the needs and contracts are created to provide structure in the helping process, many people will require further help to find and connect with resources in the church and communities. The purpose of Stage Four is to recognize the importance of advocacy and resource linkage in the PCSW process of providing care. With Stage Four in mind, special efforts must be made by pastors, church staff, to contact social workers in their community and to solicit their help in compiling listings of all available resources, appropriate for the people whom the pastors will refer to community agencies.

The tasks accomplished at this stage are illustrated in the first case study taken from Chapter One and from related ministry goals discussed in Chapter Seven for the "*Sally and Joseph's Family Crisis*" case study. The case involves the loss of Sally and Joseph's son from drug overdose, other personal and family issues. The parents' situation in the case study is unique in that neither of them requested help from the pastor. The pastors became involved during a hospital visitation, but the family's need for "advocacy" and "resource linkage" was not fully realized until the children's pastor received a creative plea for help from the youngest member of the family. In the case study, the little boy begged his pastor to allow him to remain at church so as not to return to a home so filled with sadness. With the boy's cry for help, the pastor had to decide whether to advocate on the boy's behalf. Sally and Joseph's family needs were well beyond the scope of pastoral care. Review the ministry goals below to see areas where the family might benefit from the PCSW Model, and in doing so, you should be able to distinguish between the roles of pastors and social workers.

Ministry Goals:
1. To offer help to the parents towards finding resources to meet the family's needs related all aspects of the death of their son.
2. To support the family in their efforts to reach spiritual, psychological and physical wellness.
3. To help the family to connect with spiritual, psychological and educational resources needed to address the challenges the children face

Church Resources:
1. Pastoral support, if desired, for funeral service and burial of Joey
2. Pastoral care and support, if desired, for each family member for spiritual and emotional strengthening
3. Children and young Adult programs to connect the children socially and spiritually with children in their age range
4. Outreach care for the family (i.e., meals, respite care, or house cleaning).

Outside Resources:
1. Bereavement care and Funeral Arrangements - Funeral Home
2. Psychological/psychiatric assessments (for Sally) from a professional counseling center
3. Medical care (for Sally) from a medical center
4. Psychological assessment to address anxiety (for Sara) from a professional counseling center
5. Professional grief counseling (for the entire family) from a professional counseling center
6. Follow-up services/Educational assessment and support services (for John) from a school system or private educational assessment center
7. Tutoring Services/ homework assistance (for John) from School system
8. Case management (to assist the family) with coordination of resources from a Social Service Center
9. Financial Planning/Assessment to address funeral and hospital costs from public or private financial counseling center

Stage Five: Collaboration for Transition and Change

Once the tasks set for stages One through Four of the PCSW are accomplished, then those of Stages Five and Six should be approached with the knowledge that it is at the fifth stage that individuals, families or community groups are expected to concentrate on carrying out their plans with respective activities established in the contracts during Stage Four. Stage Five is considered the working stage in the PCSW Model. Pastors and social workers might help to facilitate change in the lives of people but the people will do much of the work to bring about the change. This Stage focuses on people making "transition" from having problems to finding solutions and making internal and external "changes" that enhance their lives. For instance, if we were to consider again the case study about *"Sally and Joseph's Family Crisis,"* let's say that part of a contract for their family might include efforts to get Sally into the personal care she needs and to address her mental health issues. It is important to understand the value of linking the family with appropriate and affordable mental health services. Again, at this stage, the family might need help in learning effective use of the resources which they discovered during Stage Four. This stage in the PCSW Model is called "Transition and Change" because it reflects movements from a state of great need to one wherein the needs are met. Stage Five includes the word "change" because it captures that which occurs when people are able to turn their lives and life circumstances around for the better.

The primary focus of this stage it to carry out the implementation of the plans and contracts, this includes

- A comprehensive review of the plans and contracts
- Confirming important details of the contract

- Following through with all agreed-upon, time-sensitive steps outlined in the contract

Stage Six: Collaboration for Systematic Review of Progress

As with any effective helping model, it is crucial that the PCSW Model includes systematic reviews of the progress that is made as each task is completed. It is very important to set aside time for a strategic review of the plans and contracts that were developed and to evaluate how effectively individuals, families and communities are able to benefit from their participation in the PCSW helping process. During this stage, people who are in need, pastors as well as social workers will be able to realize the levels of progress resulting from their combined efforts. After the reviews are completed, necessary adjustments should be made to the plans and contracts to increase each individual and family or community's chances for success.

The review process requires that the contacts include measureable objectives and activities. In Sally's case, for instance, a contract might include obtaining psychological assessments of her mental status or grief counseling sessions to help her to cope with the loss of her son. There is a need to find measurable ways to determine whether the coping strategies Sally employs are effective within a reasonable time frame.

Stage Seven: Collaboration in Making Transition Decisions

After completing the tasks set for Stage Six, the next stage involves making decisions about whether to continue according to the plans and contracts or to make further changes to strategies employed, or other aspects of the work being accomplished with the help of PCSW. People seeking help from pastors will benefit from the collaborative efforts that ensure that their needs—personal, spiritual and social—are addressed holistically. At the Seventh Stage, decisions are made either to move towards closure in the PCSW relationship or to make appropriate referrals to other types of services. Once the tasks of Stage Six are accomplished, it will be necessary to make decisions as to where to go from there. This stage is very important in that it prepares those we help to recognize that success in life involves constant changes and development. Once all the problems listed in the plans and contracts are addressed sufficiently, the individuals and families or communities helped will need to continue independently within the path of success. We used the term "transition" again to signify that the tasks set for accomplishment in Stage Six need to be maintained or consciously fulfilled to ensure continued success.

Stage Eight: Collaboration for Celebration at Closure

At this final stage, special emphasis is placed on celebrating each individual, family, and community's accomplishments and the overall benefits of the PCSW Model are stressed. At Stage Eight, pastors and social workers might find ways to collaborate in celebrating the successes. Take, for instance, the case study entitled, "*What if he kills her?*" about Janet, a victim of domestic violence. It is conceivable that Janet would be willing to participate in a final pastoral care session that is dedicated solely to celebrating her spiritual growth, freedom from abuse, and her new outlook on life. Such might also be the case with her social worker at their final session. Janet could share information about her celebration in the pastoral care session and recount her success in relation to her personal and family life. By linking both settings and utilizing the collaborative approach at the Celebration and Closure Stage, Janet would be able to connect within her mind, the church and community resources that were so vital to her being able to overcome her personal and family challenges. The move towards closure of the formalized pastoral care and social work sessions that addressed domestic violence, in Janet's case would be marked by collaborative celebration.

Conclusion

With growing concerns over the numbers of people in society who will be turning to churches and other Christian organizations for help, there is a need for new and innovative strategies such as the PCSW Model to match the needs. As suggested, one possible solution is to increase collaboration between pastors and social workers. Each profession brings its own history, knowledge, values and skill in responding to the spiritual, personal and social problems people face. As collaborators in the delivery of services, pastors and social workers could develop powerful and strategic alliances, thereby creating greater opportunities to fulfill the Great Commission. The PCSW Collaboration Model is designed to increase the effectiveness of workers and ministers who address spiritual, personal and social issues affecting people in our churches and communities. In the upcoming chapter, readers have more opportunities to explore other issues that are facing the church and society as well as the benefits of the PCSW Model.

Chapter 9

Benefits of Collaboration for Other Issues Addressed in Church Settings

*"For God is not unjust; he will not forget your work
and love you have shown him as you have helped
his people and continue to help them."*
Hebrews 6:10

The whole purpose of developing the PCSW Model you see in Chapter Eight is to offer pastors and social workers a practical and biblically sound method of interfacing their ministry and work. The above verse from Hebrews 6 reminds us of God's faithfulness and His vigilant watch over our works, especially works that are motivated by love for people who look to the Christian faith as their source of strength and hope. The Bible verse also affirms our overarching beliefs, which we have shared, in the form of theological reflections throughout previous chapters, indicating that the good works of the church exalt the name of Christ.

There are many personal and social problems beside those presented in the case studies which we covered in previous chapters. Take, for instance, these challenges that pastors might encounter within church ministries: teenage pregnancies; juvenile delinquencies and arrests; parenting and educational needs of children with special needs; child development and family issues related to absentee fathers; eating disorders; and personal and social needs of elderly people who might be lacking family support.

As much as we would like to be able to say that such problems are rare among families in churches, we cannot. There is one thing that we do know--

Trouble respects no one. Regardless of people's cultural, educational, and socioeconomic backgrounds, they will encounter life's challenges. It is therefore imperative that, as Christians, we remain vigilant in our efforts to reach out to those who are facing troubles, and use the most effective means at our disposal in doing so. The PCSW Model calls for exactly that; it offers a systematic way for pastors to address problems in their churches with added help from professional social workers, especially those called to church social work. Regardless of the nature of the personal and social problems, the PCSW Model serves as a useful resource for pastors to use when they find that the knowledge and skills required to address problems of people in churches are beyond the purview of pastoral care.

Even though so far we have primarily been presenting the Model from the vantage point of pastors in church settings, social workers (as well as others) might find the Model useful for engaging church leaders. Some clients might identify to social workers their family, pastors or churches while describing their natural resources or support systems. In such cases social workers who find the need to refer clients for pastoral care might choose to introduce the PCSW Model to pastors. Take for example, the case study from Chapter Three entitled, *"Luke's Battle with AIDS: He died before he died."*

Luke is a man who is reportedly dying of AIDS-related health issues. He has a history of turning to his church, having found it to be a place of comfort and strength. A social worker helping Luke would have much to tap into if he or she were to take full advantage of natural resources available to him in her church setting. Luke raised many questions about the Christian faith, including confusion and doubt about life-and-death experiences. It is well within the scope of pastoral care for Luke to address those questions to his pastor; only the pastor was not aware of his needs. Luke expressed suicidal thoughts. A social worker working collaboratively with Luke and his pastor in this specific case might prove to be ideal. The PCSW Model helps the pastor in connecting Luke immediately to resources that addresses his sufferings.

Any social worker who is interested in employing the PCSW Model might consider offering Luke the opportunity to link the resources available in his church setting with those available in the broader community. Social workers are able to use specialized knowledge and understanding about the history, traditions, values, family systems, of the people they serve. Social workers are trained to apply culturally competent skills in an effort to apply their helping techniques with careful attention to the importance of the role of religion in people's lives.

Conclusion

Regardless of the severity and nature of the personal or social problems in society, the PCSW Model offers a step-by-step process to facilitate necessary changes and resolutions for individuals, families and communities. Developing supportive networks in churches and across communities requires creativity on the part of both pastors and social workers who endeavor to use the PCSW Model.

CHAPTER 10

Trends in Pastoral Care and
Church Social Work

*"It was he, who gave some to be apostles, some to be prophets,
some to be evangelists, and some to be pastors and teachers,
to prepare God's people for works of service, so
that the body of Christ may be built up."*
Ephesians 4:11-12

What Has Been Happening in Pastoral Care?

A number of the recent trends in pastoral care have been influenced by various cultural shifts. One shift has been the rise of post-modernity. Two influential characteristics of this shift are a movement from rational propositions to personal narratives and a movement from the universal to the local and contextual. This has resulted in a trend that is not necessarily new, but it definitely has been heightened. There is now more emphasis "on oral recounting of individual story with a focus on experience within local context at particular and crucial moments."[1] Pastors are required to develop and expand their listening skills so they can hear the needs of care-seekers and understand their specific context.[2]

A second cultural shift has been the increased recognition of multicultural communities in the U.S. This shift requires caregivers and other community leaders to become more knowledgeable and sensitive to the various ethnic characteristics present in their community. There are a couple of trends related to this shift. The first trend is that pastors are becoming better, more knowledgeable students of culture, especially cultures within their community. This means developing skills in community exegesis and engagement. The second trend is the expectation for many pastors to learn to network with various organizations that have connections with or understanding of specific ethnic groups in the community. This helps the pastor either to understand the cultural uniqueness of a person he or she is serving or to refer the person to an organization that has this understanding.

The third shift is reflected in the movement from familial influence to communal influence. Again, this is not a new phenomenon, but something that has been heightened in recent years. Emmanuel Y. Lartey, professor of pastoral theology, care and counseling at Emory University's Chandler School of Theology, stated,

> "We have to find ways of "entering creatively" into the passion and pathos not only of individuals and small groups but also of whole communities—structures and systems. Persons are deeply affected by the inter-relationships they develop within their communities. Persons are thus affected, for good or ill, by the state of health or disease of the communities they are a part of."[3]

The recent shifts are challenging pastors to recognize that meeting the needs of an individual often requires dealing with community issues that are related to or even reinforcing the individual's needs or problems. For example, a teenager's hostile feelings and behaviors towards another teenager of a different ethnicity might be a result of a community issue of racism. For a pastor to help this teenager, he or she might need to be proactive in also addressing the community's issue.

The last shift is not so much of a cultural one, but a shift that has occurred in the church community. In the last couple of decades, there have been major shifts in the image or role of the pastor. It has been a movement from shepherds, who know everyone in the congregation intimately and are always available to them, to the leaders casting vision, creating dynamic ministries, empowering others to service and managing complex organizations. As a result, pastors are collaborating with others in the congregation to care for the needs of those within the church. Three main approaches are being employed in this collaboration. The first is the training of a group of congregants to carry out the pastoral care duties in the church. These people are selected, trained, and affirmed as care ministers in the church. There is a variety of training curriculums being used by churches. Stephen Ministries[4] and Light University[5] are two examples of training courses.

The second approach utilizes the small groups of a church to carry out pastoral care. Since many churches have adopted small groups in their approach to ministry, it is natural for them to use the small group leaders and members to care for the individuals within a specific small group. For instance, if someone was dealing with grief related to the death of a family member, the small group leader and members would care for him or her and help him or her adjust to the loss.

The final approach is the hiring of staff members who are trained social workers. A simple Google search of church staff members with a MSW degree resulted in almost 6,000 hits. That number does not mean that 6,000 churches have hired someone with a MSW, but many might have hired trained social workers to meet the needs of the congregation and its community. The hiring of these individuals has also increased the collaboration with other community organizations whose expertise might be medical, educational, cultural, economic, social, or psychological.

What Has Been Happening in Church Social Work?

For several decades, the journal called *Social Work & Christianity* has been tracking the latest developments in church social work, and more indirectly, trends in pastoral care that intersects, with social services. In 2007, for instance, the Journal dedicated one of its special issues, with editors Cheryl Brandsen and Beryl Hugen, to exploring the integration of faith and social work practice. The editors introduced the special issue with an article entitled, *"Social Work through the Lens of Christian Faith."* In that issue, they described how in 2004 and 2006, groups of social work educators and practitioners converged on the campus of Calvin College to work on fostering deeper integration of faith in social work practices. Brandsen and Hugen reported that

> "Various strands of Christianity were represented at the meeting—Anglican, Baptist, Catholic, Episcopalian, and Christian-Reformed. In addition, present at the table were secular and faith-based universities, colleges, and other organizations. Although the groups varied in terms of membership, the defining purpose of each seminar was to explore foundational and enduring questions in the social work profession through the lens of the Christian faith. A large part of this work involved thinking about what it means to integrate our faith with practice: What models are available to us in this process of thinking Christianly (sic) about our work? What does it mean to do Christian scholarship in the field of social work?"[6]

All of the issues we have discussed in the preceding chapters of this book are currently challenging church social workers and church leaders, as well as other concerned members of Christian communities. In fact, the literature is replete with research findings that suggest that the social problems we face are pressing and will continue to require multiple disciplinary responses well into the future. Take, for example, the problem of domestic violence, which we addressed in Chapter Four of this book, in recognizing the seriousness of the challenges for the Christian community. In 2009, the Journal of Social Work &

Christianity published another special issue edition wherein expert guest editors, Marciana Popescu and Rene Drumm, called for authors to submit articles within the theme, "Religion, Faith Communities, and Intimate Partner Violence.[7] In yet another 2009 volume, the Journal of Social Work & Christianity's authors called attention to "elder mistreatment" and the church. Editors Michael E. Sherr and James W. Ellor dealt with that issue, which merits much more attention than we were able to give it in this book. They argued that "social workers, clergy, and congregations need to work together to address the challenges presented by elder abuse in our society."[8] For several years, the Journal has been addressing the need for more collaboration, which we have made the focus in this book. Take, for example, the titles of some articles that are recommended by the North American Association of Christian in Social Work. Experts in church social work wrote each article: *Belief systems in faith-based human services programs: A research brief,* written by Garland, D., Netting, E., O'Connor, M.K., and Yancey, G. in 2004; *When the service delivery system is a congregation.* Authored by Garland, D. in 2003; and *Is the Newer Deal a better deal? Government funding of faith-based social services,* authored by Vanderwoerd, Jim R. in 2002.[9]

With this book, we have also sought to focus attention on the integration of faith and social work practice. The unique perspective we offer is our step-by-step PCSW Model for better collaboration between pastors and social workers. Throughout the entire writing process, we have focused strongly on the pastoral care perspective as we made our argument for the benefits of synergistic collaborations with social workers in church and community settings.

Conclusion

In considering trends in pastoral care and social work, we have found that the literature spanning both disciplines has much to offer. As readers continue to explore the literature, they have the option to decide whether the questions we have raised in this book are legitimate ones. Many scholars have been calling for innovation ministries that address social problems that affect the church and society. We have sought to explore whether church leaders today are grasping the implications of how the social, economic and political changes that have been taking place in society are impacting how their ministries are carried out. Yet, we have done more than raise questions; we have offered some possible solutions.

CHAPTER 11

Job Ads and Descriptions for Pastors and a Church Social Worker

"Each one should use whatever gift he has received to serve others, faithfully administering God's grace in its various forms." Peter 4:10

Introduction

As a pastor of a small church in Canada, I (Pastor Grenz) had the privilege of hiring a Christian social worker who joined our church staff. Judy had worked for many years as a professional social worker in various social agencies. When we met, she was in the midst of a five-year leave from work because she and her husband had a child. Transitioning from secular social work practice, into church ministry Judy had her ups and downs. However, she quickly became a great help to people in our congregation and began to help us to reach out into the surrounding community. Part of our challenge was figuring out a job description, in context of the church, for Judy. Over the first six months to a year, we had regular conversations about the best way to maximize her skills and gifts for the benefit of our congregation and our mission. Once we had established her job description and Judy began expressing more understanding of the church environment, our collaborative relationship flourished. Our collaborative work was similar to that described in the case study of Chapter Seven.

Readers might recall the main case study in Chapter Seven, concerning Christ Community Church (CCC). CCC was presented as a church where new pastors could go to learn the synergic approach to pastoral care ministries. The CCC's pastoral team is comprised of a senior pastor, several associate pastors, and support staff members. The pastoral team in that case study worked together to develop "ministry goals" and to enumerate resources both within and outside the church settings to address the needs of people they served. Members of the CCC team embraced the spiritual principle of synergism in pastoral care. Now that we have recapped salient details concerning the case study, *Case Study Exercise: Pastor Moss' Synergistic Workshop*, we want readers to imagine what job descriptions might contain should leaders in a church like the CCC decide to hire pastors who will be expected to utilize the PCSW Model. We will also examine what a job description might include for a social worker in an outside organization' counseling center and who is expected to utilize the PCSW Model.

Pastors Needed:

Christ Community Church seeks candidates for two pastoral appointments. The ideal candidates will each
- Demonstrate a pastor's heart and servant leadership skills to give direction and leadership to the church.
- Have a solid history of providing pastoral care to the youths or adults in Christian communities.
- Help us as a church to fulfill the "Great Commission."
- Demonstrate ability to strengthen and encourage followers of Jesus in their walk with the Lord.
- Work collaboratively with professionals from other community-based organizations and develop and maintain contact with a network of people who provide social service resources.
- Be responsible for the direction, development and oversight of pastoral care ministries and align youth or adult ministries with the church's mission and vision statements.
- Possess the interpersonal skills needed to serve on a pastoral team that reports to the senior pastor
- Give oversight to the ministries that utilize the PCSW Model.
- Preach occasionally and to teach regularly.
- to be available to provide counsel and care as required.
- Give oversight to the small group ministry (Life Groups).

Social Worker Needed:

The Fiat Lux Counseling Center (FLCC) is looking to employ a strong candidate for a full time position as a social worker. FLCC is a private non-profit organization that was founded in 1989. The organization provides professional counseling from a Christian perspective. We have two offices staffed by four social workers. We have two positions open in our new Orlando and Tampa, Florida, locations. Our Counselees come from up to a 75-mile radius from each office because of the limited number of providers who apply the Christian emphasis. Most of the counselees we serve attend local churches. We welcome counselees of all faiths who are interested in counseling from the Christian perspective. We collaborate with local pastors to help meet the needs of their parishioners.

Consultation, assessment and practical assistance are offered on a fee-for-service basis with sliding scales applied. In addition to church social work, successful candidates will interface with case managers in community agencies. With this collaborative approach, churches pool their resources to aid those who are facing hardships. Instead of churches addressing all the social needs of those they serve, they refer some people to FLCC so our professional social worker can assist with services. FLCC receives support from local church communities and other area professionals. We receive referrals from area psychiatrists, physicians, attorneys, pastors and other professionals. In addition to professional counseling, we offer and co-sponsor marriage and family conferences. FLCC is seeking a strong candidate for a full-time position as social worker/mental health therapist.

Requirements:
Minimum MSW degree, state licensure to practice independently, five years experience is preferred. Also essential is a strong desire to work in a practice that primarily serves Christian communities. Successful candidates will meet the minimum requirement which is a Masters Degree in a Clinical Social Work program accredited by the Council on Social Work Education, with state licensure to practice independently, and desire to work in a practice serving primarily a Christian population. Competency with families, couples and individuals; issues like homelessness, substance abuse and dependency, depression, anxiety, grief, marital, parenting, life stress, sexual assault and domestic violence.

At FLCC, our mission is to integrate and utilize the faith and values of Christian counselees in the counseling process. FLCC offers a rich work environment that fosters collaboration between pastoral care and social work.

Conclusion

No ministry or profession is capable of training workers to deal with every single problem that they might encounter in the operations of their duties. From time to time, workers or ministers will say that there is no one on their team who is trained to deal with this or that. Ministers and other professionals could pray and seek guidance, but at times more than just prayer is required. Fervent prayer will indeed avail much, but much more will be accomplished when prayer is coupled with knowledge and skills. In other words, "Faith without works is dead." This book is a testament of the commitment, of us both as authors, to extend ministry beyond the walls of churches and to show our respect for persons called into social work and pastoral care. Our collaborative relationship as a pastor and a social worker is also reflective of our determination not to just *talk the talk* but to *walk the talk* so to speak.

As mentioned earlier, in the preface, many hours, days and weeks over a two-year period were spent in prayer and labor in order to produce for readers a written record of the series of conversations that transpired concerning the pressing social problems that students of pastoral care and church social work will encounter in ministries. With some degree of vulnerability, we have shared the details of our exploration of the social, political and economic changes that are taking place in society and challenges which such changes have posed for those of us serving Christian ministries.

In this as well as the two remaining chapters, efforts were made to address questions readers might have concerning the educational and training background that is needed to prepare someone to work as a pastor or social worker in settings that might employ the PCSW Model.

CHAPTER 12

Credibility and Integrity in Training and Education Resources

"Live as if you were to die tomorrow.
Learn as if you were to live forever." Mahatma Gandhi

Introduction

People of all cultures recognize the need to pass on knowledge and skill from one generation to another. Formal and informal education systems are invaluable to society's survival. Gandhi, remembered for his call for global awareness of the need for social justice, could not avoid heralding a similar call for the pursuit of learning. If pastors and social workers are to work together effectively, each will need to develop understanding of the others' training and skills. The Old Testament records a story portraying Daniel and his three colleagues as some of the most learned scholars of their time. When confronted with rapid social and political changes in a Persian society, they dedicated themselves to grasping the implications of how the socio-political changes would impact their lives and the lives of people around them. In carrying out the Lord's work, the men assumed a proactive posture in relation to all the social and cultural changes they experienced and in doing so left a good example for us to follow in our day. The story goes on to illustrate how Daniel and his friends opened up their hearts and minds to learn about the shifting culture and environment in which they found themselves. As we consider the PCSW Model, we anchor some of our thoughts in the teachings of Daniel 1:17: *"To these four young men God gave knowledge and understanding of all kinds of literature and learning."*

When reviewing the PCSW Model, one should not assume that church social workers will be fully aware of the expertise of pastors or vice-versa. In order to offer information about each discipline, we have compiled valuable information from ministry and professional organizations that support each field of work. We begin with the educational background for pastors.

Pastoral Care Education

Though the educational background varies among pastors, the collaborative model is strengthened when a pastor has a broad educational background that includes specific training in pastoral care as well as community analysis and outreach. The Master of Divinity (MDiv) degree continues to meet the educational requirements for effective collaboration. Most MDiv degrees have a strong foundation of Bible and theology, with various courses in pastoral care, preaching, leadership, and outreach. The Association of Theological Schools[1] (ATS) states, "The MDiv program should provide a breadth of exposure to the theological disciplines as well as a depth of understanding within those disciplines. It should educate students for a comprehensive range of pastoral responsibilities and skills by providing opportunities for the appropriation of theological disciplines, for deepening understanding of the life of the church, for ongoing intellectual and ministerial formation, and for exercising the arts of ministry."[2] ATS requires that this degree be the equivalent of a minimum of three academic years of full-time work.

In addition to the MDiv degree, a unit or two of Clinical Pastoral Education[3] (CPE) is very helpful for pastors. CPE is an interfaith professional training program for those preparing for ministry. "It brings theological students and ministers of all faiths (pastors, priests, rabbis, imams and others) into supervised encounter with persons in crisis. Out of an intense involvement with persons in need, and the feedback from peers and teachers, students develop new awareness of themselves as persons and of the needs of those to whom they minister. From theological reflection on specific human situations, they gain a new understanding of ministry."[4] Each CPE unit is 10-12 weeks long and can be done along with an MDiv degree.

Social Work Education

It is important to note that social workers employ a "generalist approach" that enables them to serve individuals, families, organizations and communities.[5] The ability to respond and provide services across all those client systems, or levels, is what is referred to as a "generalist approach" in social work.[6] "Social workers are able to utilize social work theories and methods for the diagnosis, treatment, and prevention of psychosocial dysfunction, disability, or impairment, including emotional, mental, and behavioral disorders." Social Workers' expertise also includes broader knowledge of community resources for referrals and services. Social workers are accessible to clients for non-emergency and emergency situations. Clinical social work is a state-regulated professional practice. State laws and regulations guide the profession. In most instances, clinical social workers are required to have the following credentials: a master's degree from a social work program accredited by the Council on Social Work Education, a minimum of two years or 3,000 hours of post-master's degree experience in a supervised clinical setting with clinical license in the state of practice."[7]

With their generalist perspective, social workers address problems while at the same time maintaining focus on how problems might be affecting individuals, families, organizations, communities and the inter-connective relationship between each of those entities.[8] Take, for example, someone who is homeless, social workers will address such a problem on the personal, and family as well as community levels.

CHAPTER 13

Ordination, Licensure, Codes of Ethics and Values

Pastors' Ordination

Many Christian denominations practice some form of ordination. Ordination is the process of setting aside or consecrating a person who the community believes has been called to minister in a particular role. This process examines and affirms the call, preparedness, beliefs, and maturity of a person to become the pastor of a church. There is no one process of ordination. Each denomination has its own process, with some having a uniform, specific structure and requirements while others might simply use suggested guidelines. The following are two examples of denominational guidelines for the ordination process for those serving as pastors. The United Methodist Church has the following requirements for ordination:

1. Certified candidate for minimum of one (1) year, maximum twelve (12) years
2. One (1) year in service ministry
3. Completion of one-half of the basic graduate theological studies to be eligible for commissioning
4. Health certificate completed by medical doctor
5. Written and oral doctrinal exam and written autobiographical statement
6. Interview and recommendation by three-fourths vote of district committee
7. Interview and recommendation by the board or ordained ministry
8. Election to provisional membership by clergy session[1]

The ordination process for most Baptist denominations is not as structured as the one above because the *denomination* does not ordain people. Ordination is a matter for the local church to exercise, though most will seek the assistance of pastors and church leaders of sister churches. When it comes to educational background, some churches require seminary training while others might not. Though there are no official guidelines, there are some common practices among most Baptist churches. The following are some of the common practices:

1. The local church calls together a council inviting pastors and church leaders from sister churches to attend
2. The council interviews the person, reviewing his or her testimony of salvation, pastoral calling from the Lord, qualifications for pastoral ministry (including theological preparation and scriptural qualifications according to 1 Timothy 3:1-7 and Titus 1:7-9)
3. Following the interview, the council makes a recommendation to the local church concerning the person's fitness for ordination
4. Based upon that recommendation, the local church typically decides whether ordination is appropriate.

Similar to ordination, there is no set code of ethics for pastors.[2] Some denominations or conventions of churches[3] have developed a code of ethics that they require or encourage a pastor to sign. Instead of providing set codes of ethics, some use this suggested list of categories when creating a code of ethics:

1. The minister's relationship with God
2. The minister's relationship with self
3. The minister's relationship with family
4. The minister's relationship with the congregation
5. The minister's relationship with co-workers (i.e., other pastoral staff and support staff)
6. The minister's relationship with other colleagues from other churches or Christian organizations
7. The minister's relationship with the community (e.g., social and municipal agencies, and schools)

Social Work Licensure

Licensed clinical social workers (LCSW) are trained to conduct psychotherapy. With the LCSW or State's equivalent licensure, social workers are qualified to help people deal with mental health issues and other life challenges. Social workers usually possess a master's degree in social work with studies in sociology, human growth and development, mental health theory and practice, human behavior/social environment, psychology, and research methods.[4] The Association of Social Work Boards (ASWB) is a regulatory organization that oversees social work profession in the U.S.[5]

The National Association of Social Workers (NASW) is the organization to consult regarding information on the credibility and integrity of the educational background of social workers. NASW indicates that

> "Social workers are our nation's leading experts when it comes to addressing some of the most serious needs of individuals and families, including those in crisis due to domestic violence, alcohol and substance abuse. In fact, Clinical social workers represent the largest group of behavioral health practitioners in the nation. Often they are the first to diagnose and treat people with mental disorders and various emotional and behavioral disturbances. Clinical social workers are essential to a variety of client-centered settings, including community mental health centers, hospitals, substance use treatment and recovery programs, schools, primary health care centers, child welfare agencies, aging services, employee assistance programs, and private practice settings [and churches]."[6]

In 1996, a NASW Delegate Assembly met and approved the following Professional Core Values and accompanying Principles of Ethics. The Assembly met again in 2008 and updated the Core Values with corresponding Ethical Principles for each value as shown below:

Social Work Values and Corresponding Ethical Principles

(1) *Service*: Social workers' primary goal is to help people in need and to address social problems. Social workers elevate service to others above self-interest.

(2) *Social justice*: Social workers challenge social injustice. Social workers pursue social change, particularly with and on behalf of vulnerable and oppressed individuals and groups of people. Social workers' social change efforts are focused primarily on issues of poverty, unemployment, discrimination, and other forms of social injustice. Social workers strive to ensure access to needed information, services, and resources; equality of opportunity; and meaningful participation in decision-making for all people.

(3) *Dignity and worth of the person*: Social workers respect the inherent dignity and worth of the person. Social workers treat each person in a caring and respectful fashion, mindful of individual differences and cultural and ethnic diversity. Social workers promote clients' socially responsible self-determination. Social workers seek to enhance clients' capacity and opportunity to change and to address their own needs.

(4) *Importance of human relationships*: Social workers recognize the central importance of human relationships. Social workers understand that relationships between and among people are an important vehicle for change. Social workers seek to strengthen relationships among people

in a purposeful effort to promote, restore, maintain, and enhance the well-being of individuals, families, social groups, organizations, and communities.

(5) *Integrity*: Social workers behave in a trustworthy manner.

(6) *Competence:* Social workers practice within their areas of competence, develop, and enhance their professional expertise. Social workers continually strive to increase their professional knowledge and skills and to apply them in practice. [7]

North American Association of Christians in Social Work

The North American Association of Christians in Social Work (NACSW) is an excellent professional organization to consult when seeking information about the progress social workers have made towards the integration of Christian faith in social work practices. NACSW is an interdenominational and international organization that began in 1950. The organization's mission statement includes these five tenets that emphasize the calling of Christian social workers:

- A dynamic relationship exists between the Christian life and social work practice. Christians in social work ought not to be motivated by temporal wealth, power or security.
- Christians in social work ought to examine and evaluate all human   ideologies and social work theories and methods as to their consistency with the Bible, their consciences, social laws, and professional codes of   ethics.
- Christians in social work ought to work for the temporal and eternal well-being of all human beings, and for the redemption of human communities and social institutions.
- Christians in social work ought to support and submit themselves to the highest standards of professional education, practice, and ethics.
- Christians in social work ought to use the insights of their faith in helping people, and to treat everyone as Jesus Christ would have them treated. [8]

Conclusion

The completion of this book is a testament to the authors' commitment to the collaborative approach and their respect for people serving in the fields of social work and pastoral care. The book also reflects the authors' determination to *walk the talk,* so to speak. As mentioned in the preface, many hours, days and weeks over a two-year period have been spent prayerfully laboring to produce for readers a text that captures the series of conversations the authors have had concerning the benefits and challenges ministry students and church social workers will encounter in Christian ministries. It is with some vulnerability that the authors have shared their view, and explored with readers implications of social, political and economic challenges of our society. Readers explored some of the struggles that churches and church leaders might face in their churches and communities. Readers might recall that the conversation began with some basic questions. We wondered together whether as part of the American church, we are finding ourselves in more of a proactive or reactive posture in relation to all the socioeconomic and political changes that are taking place. Our readers have the option to decide for themselves whether the question is a legitimate one. We also asked whether Christians today are grasping the implications of how some of the socioeconomic and political changes are impacting how we carry out the ministry of the gospel.

Parting Words

By the end of this book, readers might have surmised that the authors' believe that Christ has fully equipped believers with all that they need spiritually to fulfill the church's mission to the world. However, readers might agree that some people are indeed unprepared to assess fully all the changes that are taking place in society and therefore will need to learn ways to respond in order to meet the personal and social needs of those in their community. Nonetheless, all may take comfort in knowing that Christ remains sovereign and that the perfection of His work of salvation will be completed. Christ has done His part, and therefore the church is able to do her part. The PCSW Model is offered as an edifying resource for those in pastoral care ministries.

If readers continue the conversations that began in this book, then the hope and prayer is that God will richly bless all efforts they might make to work more collaboratively to address the needs of vulnerable people in our society. Christian social workers, in particular, are invited to reach out to church leaders and to share the wealth of knowledge and skills that their profession affords. Social workers who are called to *church* social work are encouraged to continue to develop relationships with church leaders that might facilitate the type of synergistic dialogues and collaborations that are necessary to create the types of networks described throughout this book. Finally, in considering the judicious words of Agnes Gonxha Bojaxhiu (Mother Teresa), which states, *"Let us touch the dying, the poor, the lonely and the unwanted according to the grace we have received and let us not be ashamed or slow to do the humble work,"* readers are encouraged to participate in deeper explorations of the noble calling of the church of Christ.

Notes

Preface

1. Darrel R. Watkins, *Christian Social Ministry* (Nashville: Broadman & Holman Publisher, 1994).

2. Matthew 28:18-20.

3. Jerome L. Gallagher, Megan Gallagher, Kevin Perese, Susan Schreiber, and Keith Watson, "A Description of State Temporary Assistance for Needy Families (TANF) Decisions as of October 1997," *The Urban Institute,* http://www.urban.org/UploadedPDF/307472_Tanf2.pdf (accessed May 10, 2010).

4. John Cawley, Mathis Schroeder, and Simon K.I., "How Did Welfare Reform Affect the Health Insurance Coverage of Women and Children?" *Health Services Research* 41, no. 2 (April 2006): 486-506. Also see: Ron Hastings, "Policy & Practice Welfare Reform, Success or Failure? It Worked," *Brookings,* March 15, 2006, http://www.brookings.edu/articles/2006/0315welfare_haskins.aspx (accessed February 8, 2010).

5. Robert, Wineburg, "The Reverend and Me: Faith Communities and Public Welfare," in *Cases In Macro Social Work Practice*, eds. David P. Fauri, Stephen P. Wernet, and F. Ellen Netting, (Needham Heights, MA: Allyn & Bacon, 2000),172-174.

6. Sarah Pulliam, "Hazy Faith-Based Future Charitable-choice funding will face challenges under the new administration," *Christianity Today* 52, no. 4 (April 2008): 16-17. According to Pullian funding will face challenges under the new administration.

7. See works of: Robert, Wineburg, "The Reverend and Me: Faith Communities and Public Welfare," in *Cases In Macro Social Work Practice*, eds. David P. Fauri, Stephen P. Wernet, and F. Ellen Netting, (Needham Heights, MA: Allyn & Bacon, 2000),172-174.; L. Weinberg, B. Cooper, and L. Fusarelli, "Education Vouchers for Religious Schools: Legal and Social Justice Perspectives," *Journal of Religion and Education* 27 (2000): 34-42.; Mark Chaves, "Congregations' Significance to American Civic Life," in *The Civic Life of American Religion*, eds. Paul Lichterman and C. Brady Potts, (Stanford: Stanford University Press, 2009), 69-81.; Mark Chaves and William Tsitsos, "Congregations and Social Services: What They Do, How They Do It, and With Whom," *Nonprofit and Voluntary Sector Quarterly* 30, no. 4 (December 2001): 660-683.; Mark Chaves and John Sutton, "Organizational Consolidation in American Protestant Denominations, 1890-1990," *Journal for the Scientific Study of Religion* 43, no. 1 (March 2004): 51-66.;and Michael Leo Owens and R. Drew Smith, "Congregations in Low-Income Neighborhoods and the Implications for Social Welfare Policy Research," *Nonprofit and Voluntary Sector Quarterly* 34 (September 2005): 316-339.

8. White House, "The Quiet Revolution - The President's Faith-Based and Community Initiative: A Seven-Year Progress Report," *Office of Faith-Based and Community Initiatives*, http://www.whitehouse.gov/government/fbci/The-Quiet-Revolution.pdf (accessed September 16, 2009).

9. The White House Office of Faith-Based and Community Initiatives will host the Innovations in Effective Compassion Conference. http://www.whitehouse.gov/ government /fbci/ (Accessed September 20, 2009).

10. President's Advisory Council on Faith-Based and Neighborhoods Partnerships, *A New Era of Partnerships: Report of Recommendation to the President*, http://www.whitehouse.gov/sites/default/files/microsites/ofbnp-council-final-report.pdf (accessed June 9, 2010).

11. Romans 5:20-21 (NIV), "The law was added so that the trespass might increase. But where sin increased, grace increased all the more, so that, just as sin reigned in death, so also grace might reign through righteousness to bring eternal life through Jesus Christ our Lord."

12. Isaiah 60:1.

Chapter 1

1. Colossians 3:1-17.
2. Malachi 3:6 and Numbers 23:19.
3. Luke 10:25-37.
4. John Nolland, *Word Biblical Commentary: Luke 9:21-18:34*, eds. Bruce M. Metzger, David A. Hubbard, and Glenn W. Barker, 59 vols. Word Biblical Commentary Series, (Dallas, TX: Word, Incorporated, 1993), 598.
5. The New International Version translates σπλαγχνίζομαι as "took pity". Other translates (ASV, NLT, KJV) use the word compassion instead of pity. The Enhanced Strong's Lexicon states that σπλαγχνίζομαι means to be moved as to one's bowels. The bowels were thought to be the seat of love. Today, we might say that the Samaritan's heart went out to the beaten man.
6. Matthew Henry, *Matthew Henry's commentary on the whole Bible : Complete and unabridged in one volume*, 2nd ed. (Peabody, MA: Hendrickson Publishers, 1991), Luke 10:25.
7. Mark 9:35.
8. Robert Greenleaf, *Servant Leadership: A Journey into the Nature of Legitimate Power and Greatness* (New York: Paulist Press, 1977), 7.
9. Ibid., 13.
10. J. Oswald Sanders, *Spiritual Leadership: Principles of Excellence for Every Believer* (Chicago: Moody Press, 2007), 24.
11. Luke 4:18-19. Jesus reading from Isaiah 61:1-2.
12. 1 Thessalonians 2:9; 2 Corinthians 6:3-13.
13. Galatians 5:6.
14. Galatians 5:13.
15. Diana S. Richmond Garland, ed. *Church Social Work: Helping the whole person in the context of the church* (St. Davids, PA: North American Association of Christians in Social Work, 1992), 6.
16. Ibid., 5-6.

Chapter 2

1. James Peoples and Garrick Bailey, *Humanity: An Introduction to Cultural Anthropology* (Thomas Wadsworth, Belmont, CA, 2006).
2. Matthew 28:19-20.
3. Wineburg, "The Reverend and Me: Faith Communities and Public Welfare."
4. Matthew 25:45.
5. Karin M. Eyrich-Garg, John S. Cacciola, Deni Carise, Kevin G. Lynch, Thomas A. McLellan, "Individual characteristics of the literally homeless, marginally housed, and impoverished in a US substance abuse treatment-seeking sample," *Social Psychiatry & Psychiatric Epidemiology* 43, no. 10 (October 2008): 831-842.
6. David P. Gushee, *The future of faith in American politics: The public witness of the evangelical center* (Waco: Baylor University Press, 2008), 255.
7. Gwen Ifill, "Divided We Stand," *Online News Hour*, November 3, 2004, http://www.pbs.org/newshour/bb/politics/july-dec04/divided_11-03.html (accessed July 16, 2010). Jim Wallis, Sojourner's President, is quoted to have said that poverty is mentioned 2,000 times in the Bible, through a quick study of the Hebrew and Greek words that have been translated "poor" or "poverty", the number is around 300.
8. Ronald Sider, *Just Generosity: A new vision for overcoming poverty in American* (Grand Rapids: Baker Books, 1999), 56-59.
9. John Stott, *Christian Mission in the Modern World* (Downers Grove: InterVarsity Press, 1975), 30,34.
10. Charles Colson, *Loving God* (Grand Rapids: Zondervan, 1983), 145.
11. Gerald L. Sittser, *Water from a Deep Well* (Downers Grove: InterVarsity Press, 2007), 62.
12. Matthew 28:12.
13. Matthew 18:21.
14. Matthew 18:22.

Chapter 3

1. The Henry J. Kaiser Family Foundation, "HIV/AIDS Policy Fact Sheet," *The Henry J. Kasier Family Foundation,* July 2007, http://www.kff.org/hivaids/upload/3029-071.pdf (accessed June 25, 2010).
2. Saddleback Church, "HIV/AIDS Initiative," *Saddleback Church*, http://www.saddleback.com/aboutsaddleback/signatureministries/hivaidsinitiative/index.html (accessed June 7, 2010).
3. Velmarie L. Albertini and Allen Barsky, "Reaching Haitian Men and Women Living With HIV/AIDS: Extension of CARE to the Haitian Community," *Target Center: Technical Assistance for the Ryan White Community* http://careacttarget.org/library/broward/HaitianFinalReport.pdf (accessed May 2, 2010).
4. Hebrews 4:16.
5. Job 4:10-31:40.
6. Wendell Hoffman and Stanley Grenz, *AIDS Ministry in the Midst of an Epidemic* (Grand Rapids: Baker Hook House, 1990).
7. Romans 8:20-21.
8. J. C. Ryle, *Sickness*, http://biblebb.com/files/ryle/PRACT15.TXT (accessed May 28, 2008).
9. Hoffman and Grenz, *AIDS Ministry in the Midst of an Epidemic*, 162-163.
10. Ibid., 163.

11. Ibid., 165.

12. Ibid., 168.

13. Ibid., 164.

14. Matthew 8:1-4; Mark 1:40-45; Luke 5:12-16.

15. Neville Richardson, "A Call for Care: HIV/AIDS Challenges the Church", *Journal of Theology for Southern Africa*, no. 125 (July 2006), 42.

16. James 3:17.

17. National Association of Social Work (NASW).

18. Velmarie L. Albertini and Allen Barsky, "Reaching Haitian Men and Women Living With HIV/AIDS: Extension of CARE to the Haitian Community."

19. Matthew 8:1-4.

Chapter 4

1. Federal Bureau of Investigation, "Uniform Crime Reports," http://www.fbi.gov/ucr/ucr95prs.htm (accessed July 16, 2010); and "Domestic Violence in the United States," *Sheboygan Area School District*, http://teachers.sheboygan.k12.wi.us/tgentine/documents/DOMESTICVIOLENCEUSA.pdf (accessed July 16, 2010).

2. Teri Randall, "Domestic Violence Begets Other Problems of Which Physicians Must Be Aware to Be Effective," *Journal of American Medical Association* 264, no. 8 (August 22, 1990): 939-940.

3. American Psychological Association, *Violence and the Family: Report of the American Psychological Association Presidential Task Force on Violence and the Family* (Washington D.C.: American Psychological Association, 1996), 10.

4. National Coalition Against Domestic Violence, *What Is Domestic Violence?* http://www.ndvh.org/get-educated/what-is-domestic-violence (accessed June 11, 2010).

5. National Coalition Against Domestic Violence, *Domestic Violence Awareness Month,* http://www.ncadv.org/takeaction/DomesticViolenceAwarenessMonth.php (accessed June 12, 2010).

6. Nancy Nason-Clark, "Christianity and the Experience of Domestic violence: What does Faith Have to Do with It?" *Social Work and Christianity*, 36 (Winter 2009): 379-393.

7. Psalm 140:1.

8. Peter T. O'Brien, *Word Biblical Commentary: Colossians-Philemon*, eds. Bruce M. Metzger, David A. Hubbard, and Glenn W. Barker, Word Biblical Commentary Series (Dallas, TX: Word, Incorporated, 1982), 223.

9. Elizabeth Rice Handford, *Me? Obey Him?: The Obedient Wife and God's Happiness and Blessing in the Home*, Rev. ed (Murfreesboro, TN: Sword of the Lord, 1994), 31,35.

10. Nienhuis, Nancy E, "Theological reflections on violence and abuse," *Journal of Pastoral Care & Counseling* 59, no. 1-2 (March 1, 2005): 109-123.

11. Tracy, Steven R. "Domestic violence in the church and redemptive suffering in 1 Peter," *Calvin Theological Journal* 41, no. 2 (November 1, 2006): 279-296.

12. Mary A. Kassian, *Women, Creation and the Fall* (Westchester, 111.: Crossway, 1990), 45.

13. Andrew T. Lincoln, *Word Biblical Commentary: Ephesians*, eds. Bruce M. Metzger, David A. Hubbard, and Glenn W. Barker, Word Biblical Commentary Series (Dallas, TX: Word, Incorporated, 1990), 372.

14. Ibid., 373.

15. In this brief discussion, we cannot address the theological appropriateness of divorce in instances of physical abuse in detail. Also, we acknowledge that remarriage is also a related issue, but discussion this remarriage is not pertinent to purpose of this chapter.

16. David Instone-Brewer, *Divorce and Remarriage in the Bible: The Social and Literary Context* (Grand Rapids, Mich.: Eerdmans, 2002), 275.

17. Ibid., 275

18. Ibid., 275

19. "If a man marries a woman who becomes displeasing to him because he finds something indecent about her, and he writes her a certificate of divorce, gives it to her and sends her from his house" (Deut 24:1).

20. Warren W. Wiersbe, *Wiersbe's Expository Outlines on the New Testament* (Wheaton, IL: Victor Books,1992), 69.

21. Diana S. Garland and David E. Garland, *Beyond Companionship: Christians in Marriage* (Philadelphia, PA: The Westminster Press, 1986), 156.

22. David Instone-Brewer, "What God has joined: what does the Bible really teach about divorce?" *Christianity Today* 51, no. 10 (October 1, 2007): 27.

23. "Creating A Safety Plan," *Florida Department of Children and Families*, http://www.dcf.state.fl.us/programs/domesticviolence/docs/EnglishSafetyPlan.pdf (accessed June 16, 2010).

24. Darrel R. Watkins, *Christian Social Ministry* (Nashville, TN: Broadman & Holman Publishers, 1994).

Chapter 5

1. Terry Muck and Harold Myra, "Seventy Exceptional Years: Graham speaks about televangelism, safeguarding against temptations, and other issues in ministry," *Christianity Today* 32, no. 17 (November 18, 1988): 14-25.

2. David Mace and Vera Mace, *What s Happening to Clergy Marriage* (Nashville Abingdon, 1980), 36-37.

3. William L. Lane, *Word Biblical Commentary: Hebrews 9-13*, eds. Bruce M. Metzger, David A. Hubbard, and Glenn W. Barker, Word Biblical Commentary Series (Dallas, TX: Word, Incorporated, 1991), 516.

4. 1 Timothy 4:3.

5. Donald A. Hagner, *Word Biblical Commentary: Matthew 1-13*, eds. Bruce M. Metzger, David A. Hubbard, and Glenn W. Barker, Word Biblical Commentary Series (Dallas, TX: Word, Incorporated, 1993), 292.

6. D. A. Carson, R. T. France, J. A. Moyter, and G. J. Wenham, eds. *New Bible Commentary: 21st Century Edition*, 4th ed. (Downers Grove, IL: InterVarsity Press, 1994), 1 Corinthians 7:29.

7. 1 Timothy 3:4-5; Titus 1:6.

8. Warren W. Wiersbe, *Wiersbe's Expository Outlines on the New Testament*, 372.

9. Warren W. Wiersbe, *The Bible Exposition Commentary* (Wheaton, IL: Victor Books, 1996, c1989), 1 Corinthians 3:5 Logos e-book.

10. Isaiah 48:17-18.

11. Matthew 14:22-25; 26:36-46; Mark 1:35; 6:46-47; 14:32-42; Luke 4:42; 6:12-13; 11:1-2; 22:39-46.

12. Sue Hartley, "Drawing the Lines of Professional Boundaries," *Renalink.* 3, no. 2 (Summer 2002): 1,8-9. "In social work dual relationships are not permitted. Such rela-

tionships involves social workers who assume a second relationship with a client that might result in conflicts for the professional carrying out his or her duties, or in the social, religious or business relationships."

Chapter 6

1. Matthew 28:16-20; 25:31-46.

2. President's Advisory Council on Faith-Based and Neighborhoods Partnerships, *A New Era of Partnerships: Report of Recommendation to the President*, http://www. whitehouse.gov/sites/default/files/microsites/ofbnp-council-final-report.pdf (accessed June 9, 2010).

3. Nathan L. Baker, "Baptist polity and para-church organizations," *Baptist History and Heritage* 14, no. 3 (July 1, 1979): 63.

4. Ibid., 63-64.

5. "Definitions of FBOs and CBOs," *FACE Toolkit*, http://www. nationalserviceresources.org/files/legacy/filemanager/download/196/F_Definitions.pdf (accessed June 17, 2010).

6. Teen Challenge USA, *The History of Teen Challenge*, http://teenchallengeusa.com/program/history.php (accessed June 16, 2010).

7. North American Mission Board. http://www.sbc.net/redirect.asp?url=http://www. namb.net (accessed June 9, 2010).

8. Catholic Charities USA. *History of the Catholic Charities Network*. http://www.catholiccharitiesusa.org/Page.aspx?pid=290 (accessed June 9, 2010).

9. Rev. Larry Snyder, president of Catholic Charities USA and David Beckmann, president of Bread for the World New Year. New Opportunities to Help America's Poor. Appeared in the Arkansas Democrat on January 13. http://www.catholiccharitiesusa. org/NetCommunity/Page.aspx?pid=757 (accessed June 9, 2010).

10. International Justice Mission, *What We Do*, http://www.ijm.org/ourwork/whatwedo (accessed June 9, 2010).

11. Ibid.

12. Ibid.

13. Salvation Army. *History*. http://www.salvationarmyusa.org/usn/www_usn_2.nsf/vw-dynamic-arrays/816DE20E46B88B2685257435005070FA?openDocument&charset =utf-8 (accessed June 9, 2010).

14. Lausanne Committee for World Evangelization, *Co-operating in World Evangelization A Handbook on Church Para Church Relationships*, (Wheaton, IL: Lausanne Committee for World Evangelization, 1983), 83.

15. Charles Harold Dodd, *The Parables of the Kingdom* (London: Nisbet & Company, 1935), 44.

16. Bertil Ekström, "The Kingdom of God and the church today," *Evangelical Review of Theology* 27, no. 4 (October 1, 2003): 292-305.

17. Stanley Grenz. *Theology for the Community of God* (Nashville: Broadman & Holman, 1994), 622.

18. Ibid., 625.

19. Ibid., 658.

20. Ibid., 661.

21. Jerry White, *The Church and the Parachurch: An uneasy marriage* (Portland: Multnomah Press, 1983), 82.

22. John Stott, "Lausanne Occasional Paper 24: Theological Preamble," *The Lausanne Movement*, http://www.lausanne.org/all-documents/lop-24.html#1 (accessed 17 June 2010).

23. Christopher P. Scheitle, "The Rise, Fall and Rise Again of the Parachurch Sector," *Economics of Religion Gateway*, http://www.religionomics.com/asrec/ASREC09 _Papers/Scheitle%20-%20Parachurch%20-%20ASREC09.doc (accessed June 17, 2010).

24. The Second Great Awakening (from the 1790s to the 1840s) was marked by an emphasis on personal piety. It arose in several places throughout the United States in various forms. In the northeast social activism was prominent, spawning abolition, temperance and suffrage groups, as well as groups committed to prison reform, care for the handicapped and mentally ill. Rev. Charles Grandison Finney (1792-1875) was a key leader who held that the Gospel not only saved people, but also was a means to reform society. In the upper south, Tennessee and Kentucky, the revival gave rise to evangelistic camp meetings. Calvinism was abandoned for the Arminian perspective of salvation through personal faith and devotional service. Protestant denominations (Presbyterian, Methodist and Baptist) were energized by the Second Great Awakening.

25. Mark Noll, *A History of Christianity in the United States and Canada* (Grand Rapids: Wm. B. Eerdmans Publishing Company, 1992), 438.

Chapter 7

1. Occupational Information Network (O*NET), *Summary Report for: 21-1021.00 - Child, Family, and School Social Workers*, http://online.onetcenter.org/link/summary/21-1021.00 (accessed June 17, 2010).

2. The Occupational Information Network (O*NET) is being developed under the sponsorship of the US Department of Labor/Employment and Training Administration (USDOL/ETA).

3. Job description adopted from Tennessee Career Information Delivery System http://tcids.tbr.edu/career_query2.php?soc=21-2011.00 (accessed July 6, 2010).

4. Job description adopted from the Occupation Information Network: http://www.vtlmi.info/oic3.cfm?occcode=21102100 (accessed July 6, 2010).

1. Gerald F. Hawthorne, *Word Biblical Commentary: Philippians*, eds. Bruce M. Metzger, David A. Hubbard, and Glenn W. Barker, Word Biblical Commentary Series (Dallas, TX: Word, Incorporated, 1983), 38.

2. George Fitchett provides a good holistic approach to assessing spiritual needs in his book *Assessing Spiritual Needs: A Guide for Caregivers* (Lima, OH: Academic Renewal Press, 2002).

Chapter 10

1. Emmanuel Y. Lartey, *Address given at the 7th Asia-Pacific Congress on Pastoral Care and Counseling, Perth, Western Australia*, July 15, 2010, http://www.icpcc. net/materials/globalvi_1.htm (accessed July 3, 2010).

2. Carrie Douehring provides a good discussion of the skills related to listening to personal narrative in her book, *The Practice of Pastoral Care: A Postmodern Approach* (Louisville, KY: Westminster/John Knox Press, 2006).

3. Emmanuel Y. Lartey, *Address given at the 7th Asia-Pacific Congress on Pastoral Care and Counseling, Perth, Western Australia.*

4. http://www.stephenministries.org (accessed July 3, 2010).

5. http://www.lightuniversity.com (accessed July 3, 2010).

6. Cheryl Brandsen and Beryl Huge, "Social Work through the Lens of Christian Faith: Working toward Integration," *Social Work & Christianity* 34 (2007): 349-355.

7. Marciana Popescu and Rene Drumm, "Religion, Faith Communities, and Intimate Partner Violence," *Social Work & Christianity* 36 (Winter 2009): 375-378.

8. Michael E. Sherr and James W. Ellor, "Elder Mistreatment and the Church: Potential Roles for Helping Professionals and Congregations," *Social Work & Christianity*, 36 (Spring 2009): 14-35.

9. Articles written by NACSW members, http://www.nacsw.org/Publications/Books Describe3.html (accessed June 29, 2010).

Chapter 12

1. The Association of Theological Schools (ATS) is a membership organization of more than 250 graduate schools in the United States and Canada that conduct post-baccalaureate professional and academic degree programs to educate persons for the practice of ministry and for teaching and research in the theological disciplines. The Commission on Accrediting of ATS accredits institutions and approves degree programs offered by accredited schools.

2. Association of Theological Schools, Degree Program Standards, www.ats.edu/Accrediting/Documents/08DegreeStandards.pdf (accessed July 2, 2010), 179.

3. Association for Clinical Pastoral Education, http://www.acpe.edu (accessed July 2, 2010).

4. Association for Clinical Pastoral Education, "What is Clinical Pastoral Education," *Frequently Asked Questions About ACPE Clinical Pastoral* Education, http://www.acpe.edu/faq.htm (accessed July 2, 2010).

5. Velmarie L. Albertini, "Social networks and community support: Sustaining women in need of community-based adult education programs," *New Directions for Adult & Continuing Education* no. 122 (Summer 2009): 23-32.

6. Charles Zastrow and Karen K. Kirst-Ashman, *Understanding Human Behavior and the Social Environment*, 7th ed. (Belmont, CA: Brooks/Cole, 2006).

7. Robert L. Barker, *The Social Work Dictionary*, 4th ed. (Washington, DC: NASW Press, 2003).

8. Trained social worker possesses either a bachelors or masters degree in social work from universities accredited by the Council on Social Work Education. This includes both secular and Christian graduate and undergraduate programs. http://www.cswe.org/Accreditation/organizations.aspx (accessed June 17, 2010).

Chapter 13

1. "Steps into Ordained Ministry," *General Board of Higher Education and Ministry*, http://www.gbhem.org/site/c.lsKSL3POLvF/b.3738647/k.CF90/Steps_into_Ordained _Ministry.htm (accessed July 3, 2010).

2. Joe Trull and James Carter provide a thorough discussion of ministerial ethics and provide various examples of codes of ethics in their book *Ministerial Ethics: Moral Formation of Church Leaders* (Baker Academic, 2004).

3. The Texas Baptist Convention has presented a good example of a Ministerial Code of Ethics, http://www.bgct.org/texasbaptists/Document.Doc?&id=3062 (accessed July 2, 2010).

4. Merriam-Webster Online Dictionary, http://www.merriam-webster.com (accessed June 17, 2010).

5. *Association of Social Work Boards*, http://www.aswb.org/index.asp (accessed March 1, 2010).

6. Robert L. Barker, *The Social Work Dictionary*.

7. National Association of Social Work, http://www.naswdc.org (accessed June 17, 2010).

8. Ibid.

BIBLIOGRAPHY

Albertini, Velmarie L. "Social networks and community support: Sustaining women in need of community-based adult education programs." *New Directions for Adult & Continuing Education* no. 122 (Summer 2009): 23-32.

Albertini, Velmarie L., and Allen Barsky. "Reaching Haitian Men and Women Living With HIV/AIDS: Extension of CARE to the Haitian Community." *Target Center: Technical Assistance for the Ryan White Community.* 2003. http://careacttarget.org/library/broward/HaitianFinalReport.pdf (accessed May 2, 2010).

American Psychological Association. *Violence and the Family: Report of the American Psychological Association Presidential Task Force on Violence and the Family.* Washington D.C.: American Psychological Association, 1996.

Association for Clinical Pastoral Education."What is Clinical Pastoral Education." *Frequently Asked Questions About ACPE Clinical Pastoral* Education. http://www.acpe.edu/faq.htm (accessed July 2, 2010).

Association of Social Work Boards. http://www.aswb.org/index.asp (accessed March 1, 2010).

Baker, Nathan L. "Baptist polity and para-church organizations." *Baptist History and Heritage* 14, no. 3 (July 1, 1979): 62-70.

Barker, Robert L. *The Social Work Dictionary*, 4th ed. Washington, DC: NASW Press, 2003.

Brandsen, Cheryl and Beryl Huge. "Social Work through the Lens of Christian Faith: Working toward Integration." *Social Work & Christianity* 34 (2007): 349-355.

Carson, D.A., R.T. France, J. A. Moyter, and G. J. Wenham, eds. *New Bible Commentary: 21st Century Edition*, 4th ed. Downers Grove, IL: InterVarsity Press, 1994.

Catholic Charities USA. *History of the Catholic Charities Network.* http://www.catholiccharitiesusa.org/Page.aspx?pid=290 (accessed June 9, 2010).

Cawley, John, Mathis Schroeder, and Kosali I Simon. "How Did Welfare Reform Affect the Health Insurance Coverage of Women and Children?" *Health Services Research* 41, no. 2 (April 2006): 486-506.

Chaves, Mark. "Congregations' Significance to American Civic Life." In *The Civic Life of American Religion*, edited by Paul Lichterman and C. Brady Potts, 69-81. Stanford: Stanford University Press, 2009.

Chaves, Mark, and William Tsitsos. "Congregations and Social Services: What They Do, How They Do It, and With Whom." *Nonprofit and Voluntary Sector Quarterly* 30, no. 4 (December 2001): 660-683.

Chaves, Mark, and John Sutton. "Organizational Consolidation in American Protestant Denominations, 1890-1990." *Journal for the Scientific Study of Religion* 43, no. 1 (March 2004): 51-66.

Cnaan, Ram A., and John DuIulio. *The Invisible Caring Hand Of American Congregations and The Provision Of Welfare*. New York, NY: New York University Press, 2002.

Colson, Charles. *Loving God*. Grand Rapids, MI: Zondervan, 1983.

Council on Social Work Education. *Directory of Accredited Programs*. http://www.cswe.org/Accreditation/organizations.aspx (accessed June 17, 2010).

"Definitions of FBOs and CBOs." *FACE Toolkit*. http://www.nationalservice resources.org/files/legacy/filemanager/download/196/F_Definitions.pdf (accessed June 17, 2010).

Dodd, Charles Harold. *The Parables of the Kingdom*. London: Nisbet & Company, 1935.

"Domestic Violence in the United States." *Sheboygan Area School District*. http://teachers.sheboygan.k12.wi.us/tgentine/documents/DOMESTICVIOLENCEU SA.pdf (accessed July 16, 2010).

Ekström, Bertil. "The Kingdom of God and the church today." *Evangelical Review of Theology* 27, no. 4 (October 1, 2003): 292-305.

Eyrich-Garg, Karin M., John S. Cacciola, Deni Carise, Kevin G. Lynch, and Thomas A. McLellan. "Individual characteristics of the literally homeless, marginally housed, and impoverished in a US substance abuse treatment-seeking sample." *Social Psychiatry & Psychiatric Epidemiology* 43, no. 10 (October 2008): 831-842.

Farnsley, Arthur E. *Rising Expectations: Urban Congregations, Welfare Reform, and Civic Life*. Bloomington, IN: Indiana University Press, 2003.

"Fast Facts on Domestic Violence." *The Clark County Prosecuting Attorney*. http://www.clarkprosecutor.org/html/domviol/facts.htm (accessed July 16, 2010).

Federal Bureau of Investigation. "Uniform Crime Reports." 1996. http://www.fbi.gov/ucr/ucr95prs.htm (accessed July 16, 2010).

Fitchett, George. *Assessing Spiritual Needs: A Guide for Caregivers*. Lima, OH: Academic Renewal Press, 2002.

Gallagher, L. Jerome, Megan Gallagher, Kevin Perese, Susan Schreiber, and Keith Watson. "A Description of State Temporary Assistance for Needy Families (TANF) Decisions as of October 1997." *The Urban Institute*. May 1998. http://www. urban.org/UploadedPDF/307472_Tanf2.pdf (accessed May 10, 2010).

Garland, Diana S. Richmond, ed. *Church Social Work: Helping the whole person in the context of the church*. St. Davids, PA: North American Association of Christians in Social Work, 1992.

Garland, Diana S. and David E. Garland. *Beyond Companionship: Christians in Marriage*. Philadelphia, PA: The Westminster Press, 1986.

Greenleaf, Robert. *Servant Leadership: A Journey into the Nature of Legitimate Power and Greatness*. New York, NY: Paulist Press, 1977.

Grenz, Stanley. *Theology for the Community of God*. Nashville, TN: Broadman & Holman, 1994.

Gushee, David P. *The Future of Faith in American Politics: The Public Witness of the Evangelical Center*. Waco: Baylor University Press, 2008.

Hagner, Donald A. *Word Biblical Commentary: Matthew 1-13*. Edited by Bruce M. Metzger, David A. Hubbard, and Glenn W. Barker, 59 vols. Word Biblical Commentary Series. Dallas, TX: Word, Incorporated, 1993.

Handford, Elizabeth Rice. *Me? Obey Him?: The Obedient Wife and God's Happiness and Blessing in the Home*, Rev. ed. Murfreesboro, TN: Sword of the Lord, 1994.

Hartley, Sue. "Drawing the Lines of Professional Boundaries." *Renalink* 3, no. 2 (Summer 2002): 1,8-9.

Hastings, Ron. "Policy & Practice Welfare Reform, Success or Failure? It Worked." *Brookings*. March 15, 2006. http://www.brookings.edu/articles/2006/0315welfare_haskins.aspx (accessed February 8, 2010).

Hawthorne, Gerald F. *Word Biblical Commentary: Philippians*. Edited by Bruce M. Metzger, David A. Hubbard, and Glenn W. Barker, 59 vols. Word Biblical Commentary Series. Dallas, TX: Word, Incorporated, 1983.

Henry, Matthew. *Matthew Henry's commentary on the whole Bible : Complete and unabridged in one volume*, 2nd ed. Peabody, MA: Hendrickson Publishers, 1991.

Hoffman, Wendell and Stanley Grenz. *AIDS Ministry in the Midst of an Epidemic*. Grand Rapids, MI: Baker Hook House, 1990.

Ifill, Gwen. "Divided We Stand." *Online News Hour*. November 3, 2004. http://www.pbs.org/newshour/bb/politics/july-dec04/divided_11-03.html (accessed July 16, 2010).

Instone-Brewer, David. "What God has joined: What does the Bible really teach about divorce?." *Christianity Today* 51, no. 10 (October 1, 2007): 26-29.

—. *Divorce and Remarriage in the Bible: The Social and Literary Context*. Grand Rapids, MI: Eerdmans, 2002.

International Justice Mission. *What We Do*. http://www.ijm.org/ourwork/whatwedo (accessed June 9, 2010).

Kassian, Mary A. *Women, Creation and the Fall*. Westchester, IL: Crossway, 1990.

Lane, William L. *Word Biblical Commentary: Hebrews 9-13*. Edited by Bruce M. Metzger, David A. Hubbard, and Glenn W. Barker, 59 vols. Word Biblical Commentary Series. Dallas, TX: Word, Incorporated, 1991.

Lartey, Emmanuel Y. *Address given at the 7th Asia-Pacific Congress on Pastoral Care and Counseling, Perth, Western Australia*. July 15, 2010. http://www.icpcc.net/materials/globalvi_1.htm (accessed July 3, 2010).

Lausanne Committee for World Evangelization. *Co-operating in World Evangelization A Handbook on Church Para Church Relationships*. Wheaton, IL: Lausanne Committee for World Evangelization, 1983.

Lincoln, Andrew T. *Word Biblical Commentary: Ephesians*. Edited by Bruce M. Metzger, David A. Hubbard, and Glenn W. Barker, 59 vols. Word Biblical Commentary Series. Dallas, TX: Word, Incorporated, 1990.

Mace, David and Vera Mace. *What s Happening to Clergy Marriage*. Nashville, TN: Abingdon Press, 1980.

Merriam-Webster Online Dictionary. http://www.merriam-webster.com (accessed June 17, 2010).

Muck, Terry and Harold Myra. "Seventy Exceptional Years: Graham speaks about televangelism, safeguarding against temptations, and other issues in ministry." *Christianity Today* 32, no. 17 (November 18, 1988): 14-25.

Nason-Clark, Nancy. "Christianity and the Experience of Domestic violence: What does Faith Have to Do with It?" *Social Work and Christianity* 36 (Winter 2009): 379-393.

National Association of Social Worker. *Codes of Ethics*. 1999. http://www.socialworkers.org/pubs/code/default.asp (accessed June 17, 2010).

National Association of Social Work. http://www.naswdc.org (accessed June 17, 2010).

National Coalition Against Domestic Violence. *Domestic Violence Awareness Month.* http://www.ncadv.org/takeaction/DomesticViolenceAwarenessMonth.php (accessed June 12, 2010).

___. *What Is Domestic Violence?* http://www.ndvh.org/get-educated/what-is-domestic-violence (accessed June 11, 2010).

Nienhuis, Nancy E. "Theological reflections on violence and abuse." *Journal of Pastoral Care & Counseling* 59, no. 1-2 (March 1, 2005): 109-123.

Noll, Mark. *A History of Christianity in the United States and Canada.* Grand Rapids, MI: Wm. B. Eerdmans Publishing Company, 1992.

Nolland, John. *Word Biblical Commentary: Luke 9:21-18:34.* Edited by Bruce M. Metzger, David A. Hubbard, and Glenn W. Barker, 59 vols. Word Biblical Commentary Series. Dallas, TX: Word, Incorporated, 1993.

North American Mission Board. http://www.sbc.net/redirect.asp?url=http://www.namb.net (accessed June 9, 2010).

O'Brien, Peter T. *Word Biblical Commentary: Colossians-Philemon.* Edited by Bruce M. Metzger, David A. Hubbard, and Glenn W. Barker, 59 vols. Word Biblical Commentary Series. Dallas, TX: Word, Incorporated, 1982.

Occupational Information Network (O*NET). *Summary Report for: 21-1021.00 - Child, Family, and School Social Workers.* 2009. http://online.onetcenter.org/link/ summary/21-1021.00 (accessed June 17, 2010).

Owens, Michael Leo and R. Drew Smith. "Congregations in Low-Income Neighborhoods and the Implications for Social Welfare Policy Research." *Nonprofit and Voluntary Sector Quarterly* 34 (September 2005): 316-339.

Peoples, James and Garrick Bailey. *Humanity: An Introduction to Cultural Anthropology.* Belmont, CA: Thomas Wadsworth, 2006.

Popescu, Marciana and Rene Drumm. "Religion, Faith Communities, and Intimate Partner Violence." *Social Work & Christianity* 36 (Winter 2009): 375-378.

Power, Samantha. "The Enforcer: A Christian lawyer's global crusade." *The New Yorker.* January 19, 2009. http://www.newyorker.com/reporting/2009/01/19/090119fa_fact_power#ixzz0qWJideev (accessed June 9, 2010).

President's Advisory Council on Faith-Based and Neighborhoods Partnerships. *A New Era of Partnerships: Report of Recommendation to the President.* March 2010. http://www.whitehouse.gov/sites/default/files/microsites/ofbnp-council-final-report.pdf (accessed June 9, 2010).

Pulliam, Sarah. "Hazy Faith-Based Future Charitable-choice funding will face challenges under the new administration." *Christianity Today* 52, no. 4 (April 2008): 16-17.

Randall, Teri. "Domestic Violence Begets Other Problems of Which Physicians Must Be Aware to Be Effective." *Journal of American Medical Association* 264, no. 8 (August 22, 1990): 939-940.

Richardson, Neville. "A Call for Care: HIV/AIDS Challenges the Church." *Journal of Theology for Southern Africa* no. 125 (July 2006): 38-50.

Ryle, J. C. *Sickness.* http://biblebb.com/files/ryle/PRACT15.TXT (accessed May 28, 2008).

Salvation Army. History. http://www.salvationarmyusa.org/usn/www_usn_2.nsf/vw-dynamic-arrays/816DE20E46B88B2685257435005070FA?openDocument&charset=utf-8 (accessed June 9, 2010).

Sanders, J. Oswald. *Spiritual Leadership: Principles of Excellence for Every Believer.* Chicago, IL: Moody Press, 2007.

Scheitle, Christopher P."The Rise, Fall and Rise Again of the Parachurch Sector." *Economics of Religion Gateway.* http://www.religionomics.com/asrec/ASREC09_Papers/Scheitle%20-%20Parachurch%20-%20ASREC09.doc (accessed June 17, 2010).

Sherr, Michael E. and James W. Ellor. "Elder Mistreatment and the Church: Potential Roles for Helping Professionals and Congregations." *Social Work & Christianity*, 36 (Spring 2009): 14-35.

Sider, Ronald J. *Just Generosity: A new vision for overcoming poverty in American.* Grand Rapids, MI: Baker Books, 1999.

Sittser, Gerald L. *Water from a Deep Well.* Downers Grove, IL: InterVarsity Press, 2007.

"Steps into Ordained Ministry." *General Board of Higher Education and Ministry.* http://www.gbhem.org/site/c.lsKSL3POLvF/b.3738647/k.CF90/Steps_into_Ordained_Ministry.htm (accessed July 3, 2010).

Stott, John. *Christian Mission in the Modern World.* Downers Grove, IL: InterVarsity Press, 1975.

___. "Lausanne Occasional Paper 24: Theological Preamble." *The Lausanne Movement.* 1980. http://www.lausanne.org/all-documents/lop-24.html#1 (accessed 17 June 2010).

The Henry J. Kaiser Family Foundation. "HIV/AIDS Policy Fact Sheet." *The Henry J. Kasier Family Foundation.* July 2007. http://www.kff.org/hivaids/upload/3029-071.pdf (accessed June 25, 2010).

Teen Challenge USA. *The History of Teen Challenge.* http://teenchallengeusa.com/program/history.php (accessed June 16, 2010).

Tracy, Steven R. "Domestic violence in the church and redemptive suffering in 1 Peter." *Calvin Theological Journal* 41, no. 2 (November 1, 2006): 279-296.

United Way. *History of United Way.* http://www.liveunited.org/about/history.cfm (accessed June 9, 2010).

Watkins, Darrel, R. *Christian Social Ministry.* Nashville, TN: Broadman & Holman Publishers, 1994.

White House. *Office of Faith-Based and Community Initiatives.* http://www.whitehouse.gov/government/fbci (accessed September 20, 2009).

___. "The Quiet Revolution - The President's Faith-Based and Community Initiative: A Seven-Year Progress Report." *Office of Faith-Based and Community Initiatives.* February 2008. http://www.whitehouse.gov/government/fbci/The-Quiet-Revolution.pdf (accessed September 16, 2009).

White, Jerry. *The Church and the Parachurch: An uneasy marriage.* Portland, OR: Multnomah Press, 1983.

Wiersbe, Warren. *The Bible Exposition Commentary.* Wheaton, IL: Victor Books, 1996, c1989. Logos e-book.

___. *Wiersbe's Expository Outlines on the New Testament.* Wheaton, IL: Victor Books, 1992.

Weinberg, L., B. Cooper, and L. Fusarelli. "Education Vouchers for Religious Schools: Legal and Social Justice Perspectives." *Journal of Religion and Education* 27 (2000): 34-42.

Wineburg, Robert. "The Reverend and Me: Faith Communities and Public Welfare." In *Cases In Macro Social Work Practice*, edited by David P. Fauri, Stephen P. Wernet, and F. Ellen Netting, 172-174 . Needham Heights, MA: Allyn & Bacon, 2000.

Zastrow, Charles, and Karen K. Kirst-Ashman. *Understanding Human Behavior and the Social Environment*, 7th ed. Belmont, CA: Brooks/Cole, 2006.

About the Authors

Velmarie Albertini, Associate Professor of Social Work at Southeastern University in Central Florida. She has served for over fifteen years in state and private universities in administrative roles as Social Work Graduate Program Coordinator and Chair of an undergraduate Christian Social Ministry Degree Program. Her areas of research and ministry include the acculturation and adjustment of Caribbean immigrants and church social work.

Jonathan Grenz, Associate Professor of Ministry Leadership Studies in the School of Ministry at Palm Beach Atlantic University in South Florida. Prior to reentering the academy, he ministered for over fifteen years, as a pastor in the U.S. and Canada.